Match of My Life

SPURS

KNOW THE SCORE BOOKS PUBLICATIONS

CULT HEROES	Author	ISBN
CHELSEA	Leo Moynihan	1-905449-00-3
MANCHESTER CITY	David Clayton	978-1-905449-05-7
NEWCASTLE	Dylan Younger	1-905449-03-8
SOUTHAMPTON	Jeremy Wilson	1-905449-01-1
WEST BROM	Simon Wright	1-905449-02-X

MATCH OF MY LIFE	Editor	ISBN
ENGLAND WORLD CUP	Massarella & Moynihan	1-905449-52-6
EUROPEAN CUP FINALS	Ben Lyttleton	1-905449-57-7
FULHAM	Michael Heatley	1-905449-51-8
LEEDS	David Saffer	1-905449-54-2
LIVERPOOL	Leo Moynihan	1-905449-50-X
SHEFFIELD UNITED	Nick Johnson	1-905449-62-3
STOKE CITY	Simon Lowe	978-1-905449-55-2
SUNDERLAND	Rob Mason	1-905449-60-7
SPURS	Allen & Massarella	978-1-905449-58-3
WOLVES	Simon Lowe	1-905449-56-9

HARRY HARRIS	Author	ISBN
WORLD CUP DIARY	Harry Harris	1-905449-90-9
HOLD THE BACK PAGE	Harry Harris	1-905449-91-7

AUTOBIOGRAPHY	Author	ISBN
TACKLES LIKE A FERRET (England Cover)	Paul Parker	1-905449-47-X
TACKLES LIKE A FERRET (Manchester United Cover)	Paul Parker	1-905449-46-1

FOOTBALL FICTION	Author	ISBN
BURKSEY The Autobiography of a Football God	Peter Morfoot	1-905449-49-6

CRICKET	Author	ISBN
MOML: THE ASHES	Pilger & Wightman	1-905449-63-1

FORTHCOMING PUBLICATIONS IN 2007

CULT HEROES	Author	ISBN
CARLISLE	Mark Harrison	978-1-905449-09-7
CELTIC	David Potter	978-1-905449-08-8
NOTINGHAM FOREST	David McVay	978-1-905449-06-4
RANGERS	Paul Smith	978-1-905449-07-1

MATCH OF MY LIFE	Editor	ISBN
ASTON VILLA	Neil Moxley	978-1-905449-65-1
BOLTON WANDERERS	David Saffer	978-1-905449-64-4
DERBY COUNTY	Johnson & Matthews	978-1-905449-68-2
FA CUP FINALS	David Saffer	978-1-905449-53-4
MANCHESTER UNITED	Brian Hughes	978-1-905449-59-0

GENERAL FOOTBALL	Author	ISBN
CHAMPIONS LEAGUE YEARBOOK	Harry Harris	978-1-905449-93-4
OUTCASTS The Lands FIFA Forgot	Steve Menary	978-1-905449-31-6
PARISH TO PLANET A History of Football	Dr Eric Midwinter	978-1-905449-30-9
MY PREMIERSHIP DIARY Reading's Season in the Premiership	Marcus Hahnemann	978-1-905449-33-0

CRICKET	Author	ISBN
GROVEL! The 1976 West IndiesTour of England	David Tossell	978-1-905449-43-9
MY AUTOBIOGRAPHY	Shaun Udal	978-1-905449-42-2
WASTED?	Paul Smith	978-1-905449-45-3
LEAGUE CRICKET YEARBOOK North West edition	Andy Searle	978-1-905449-70-5
LEAGUE CRICKET YEARBOOK North East edition	Andy Searle	978-1-905449-71-2
LEAGUE CRICKET YEARBOOK Midlands edition	Andy Searle	978-1-905449-72-9

Match of My Life

SPURS

Editors: Matt Allen & Louis Massarella

Series Editor: Simon Lowe
Know The Score Books Limited

www.knowthescorebooks.com

First published in the United Kingdom
by Know The Score Books Limited, 2007

Know The Score Books Limited
118 Alcester Road
Studley
Warwickshire
B80 7NT

www.knowthescorebooks.com

A CIP catalogue record is available for this book from the British Library

ISBN-13: 978-1-905449-58-3

Jacket and book design by Lisa David

Printed and bound in Great Britain
By Cromwell Press, Trowbridge, Wiltshire

Photographs in this book are reproduced by kind permission of: Colorsport, EMPICS

Front cover:

Top left The 1961 Double winning team show off the Championship trophy and the FA Cup after becoming the first side for 54 years

Bottom left Steve Perryman (left) and Ricky Villa parade the 1981 FA Cup after the incredible 3-2 victory over Manchester City in the replay

Bottom right Gary Mabbutt lifts the 1991 FA Cup to prove that Spurs do win when the year ends in 1!

Rear cover:

Top left Clive Allen celebrates yet another goal during his record-breaking 1986/87 haul of 49

Top left Ossie Ardiles brought a lot of glamour with him when he signed for his beloved 'Tott-ing-hsm'

Top left Garth Crooks skips past Manchester City's Nicky Reid during the 1981 FA Cup Final at Wembley, but it was his performance in the semi-final replay victory over Wolves which he has chosen as his greatest match for Spurs

Editor's Acknowledgements

Louis would like to thank all the participants for their co-operation and patience, particularly Steve Perryman for lending me his video of the game and putting Matt in touch with Ossie and Ricky. I would also like to thank Andy Porter, Simon Felstein at Spurs, Alex Stone at the FA, Funkazi Koroye, Exeter City FC, James 'Rambo' Maw, Andy 'Jonesy' Jones, my mum for lending me her car, Gracie. Most of all I'd like to thank my late nan Winifred Overton, for not letting me support Arsenal.

Matt Allen would like to say cheers to the following for their help, patience and assistance: Cliff Jones for the tea, biscuits and guided tour of White Hart Lane, Ossie and Ricky for the lunch, Bobby and Jean Smith for their kind hospitality and Terry Baker for putting me in touch with Martin Peters. I'd Also like to thank Daniel Ardiles for arranging the meeting with his dad, and Gary Mabbutt for taking the time to talk to me about the 1991 FA Cup Final. Plus Auntie Phoebe, Johnny Cigs, Mooro, Action Jackson, The Potters, Dave Croghan, Dave 'The Jackal' Simmons, Sid Freeman (fore!), the White Hart Lane Dodds, and all at Gentlemen's Wednesday five-a-side for the beer therapy. And of course mum, dad, Katie and Joanna. But especially dad, for not making me support Arsenal.

Also a big thank you to FA Cup specialist David Saffer for his invaluable help with the interviews with Pat Jennings and Dave Mackay

Matt Allen & Louis Massarella
November 2006

Contents

Introduction

Since the early nineties, supporting Tottenham Hotspur has been something a labour of love. You need only consider the euphoria that last season's ultimately heartbreaking quest for a Champions League place brought to realise how thin on the ground success had been in the last decade and a half.

For sustained periods during the sixties, seventies and eighties, fourth place would have been met with disappointment by fans, for it would have meant just scraping into the UEFA Cup, unless – as was frequently the case – Spurs won the FA Cup and a place in the now defunct, but then highly-prestigious, European Cup Winners Cup instead. Whatever the European competition, more often than not the Spurs players would meet their fans' expectations by having a decent tilt at bringing home the bacon, and three times they did just that.

My own joy, and subsequently suffering, as a Spurs supporter began on a May evening in 1984 when, as a six-year-old, I stayed up to watch the UEFA Cup Final with my dad, a Manchester United-supporting Yorkshireman who had an unlikely soft spot for Spurs because of their tradition of playing with style. I'm delighted to say the hero of that famous penalty shootout win over Anderlecht, Tony Parks, retells his story of that night in this book. As for me, I wanted to be a goalkeeper and a Spurs fan because of that night, but a lack of height soon ruled out the former while the latter was no longer a matter of choice.

I was a prolific striker in my cub team by the time I saw the flip side of following a team of inconsistent stylists; 1987 was the year, Coventry City were the opposition, and Clive Allen was the hero who scored 49 goals but ended the season with nothing but individual accolades to show for his considerable efforts. Clive also features in this book with his account of that extraordinary season. In fact, all the subjects in this book recall a game from a season in which silverware was won – or in Allen's case snatched away at the death.

These largely glorious memoirs are book-ended by Bobby Smith, the Double-winning centre-forward from 1961, and 1991 FA Cup-winning captain, Gary Mabbutt. Both were interviewed by my co-editor, Matt Allen (no relation), whose love-hate relationship with Spurs began three years earlier than mine, when Ricky Villa slalomed his way through Manchester City's defence to score perhaps the greatest FA Cup Final goal ever.

Matt's dad, an Arsenal fan, foolishly let Allen Junior decide his own allegiances at a time when it was a choice between David O'Leary and Kenny Sansom or Glenn Hoddle and Ossie Ardiles. "Why couldn't you have supported Arsenal?" Matt's dad still groans, although given that the Allens lived in Bromley, he would probably have settled for his son supporting Gillingham. Anybody but the sworn enemy.

Like myself, Matt had the pleasure of interviewing his formative footballing heroes for this book: Ricky Villa and Ossie Ardiles. That's right, Ossie and Ricky chatting about the 1981 Final(s). Together. Over dinner. The lucky blighter. But not before Matt had taken a stroll around the White Hart Lane dressing rooms and pitch as Welsh wing wizard Cliff Jones retold the remarkable story of Tottenham becoming the first British club to win a European trophy, the 1963 Cup Winners Cup.

As I mentioned earlier, this whole book is like a catalogue of Spurs triumphs. No surprise, really, given that 12 major trophies were won – with as many near misses – in the 30 years covered, and after having the pleasure of spending time with the heroes and legends who were at the centre of the action, it almost feels like we were there to witness every one of those triumphs ourselves.

Our one regret is that we can't supplement these successes with one from the past 15 years (despite Allan Nielsen's last-gasp winner, the 1999 League Cup somehow doesn't feel very memorable by comparison, despite being relatively recent). What we need now is for the current Spurs team to give us an excuse to update this book.

Louis Massarella
November 2006

Foreword

PETER EBDON

One thing you're guaranteed with Spurs matches is flair, excitement and passion. Consistency has never really been our thing in recent decades. Ever since I started supporting Tottenham as a kid growing up in north London I'd always watch us get to within touching distance of greatness before falling short, which was very frustrating, but at least we were never short of excitement.

But it was always a thrilling ride: the FA Cup wins of 1981 and 1982, not to mention our European nights from around the same time, especially the dramatic penalty shoot out of 1984 (more of which you'll read about later). Some truly great players emerged at that time too, including Ossie Ardiles, Glenn Hoddle, Steve Perryman and Ricky Villa. Many of them feature here in Match Of My Life, which relives some of the greatest games in Tottenham's history through the eyes of the players who were there, on the pitch, involved in these fantastic games.

Of course before the '80s we were a great side. Under Bill Nicholson Spurs revolutionised the way football was played in the 1960s. What followed was a period of success that saw us win the double in 1961 and enter into the European Cup the following year. With players like Bobby Smith, Cliff Jones, Greavesie, Dave Mackay and Danny Blanchflower at White Hart Lane, we ensured a legacy of greatness that meant the Spurs name was forever etched alongside the some of European greats.

But what attracted me to Tottenham when I was a kid was the style. We've always been a team that have played football with flair and imagination. And no-one epitomised that more than Glenn Hoddle, a footballer who was very much an early incarnation of the modern day player with his vision and passing ability. Sadly, though, flair is rarely twinned with League success, which explains why our Cup heritage is so strong. Because of this, many of the games relived in Match Of My Life are Cup games rather than League matches. Bobby Smith recalls the 1961 FA Cup Final against Leicester City where The Double was finally secured (a game he never should have played in due to injury). Cliff Jones, my old PE teacher at school, returns to the first ever European tie to be played out White Hart

Lane. Argentinean legends, Ricky Villa and Ossie Ardiles even take us back to the 1981 FA Cup Final, complete with Ricky's magical goal and the pop single recorded with Chas 'n' Dave.

Match Of My Life also brings together Tony Parks, Gary Mabbutt, Clive Allen, Martin Peters and Garth Crooks each one recalling their greatest ever Spurs game. For most Spurs fans, these matches have been etched into White Hart Lane folklore. Now we can relive them with the players who were actually there, playing at Tottenham during the Glory, Glory Nights.

Peter Ebdon
January 2007

BOBBY SMITH
CENTRE-FORWARD 1955–1964

BORN   22 February 1933, Skelton, Yorkshire
SIGNED   December 1955 from Chelsea; £16,000
SPURS CAREER   376 appearances, 285 goals
HONOURS   FA Cup winner 1961 & 1962; European Cup Winners'
Cup 1963
LEFT   Transferred to Brighton, May 1964; £5,000

When goalkeepers squared up to Tottenham Hotspur in the late 50s and
early 60s, they squared up to Bobby Smith: a 5'10" centre forward who
used his 12 stone 11 pound frame like a heavyweight boxer. With his
muscular build, Spurs turned from relegation candidates in the mid-1950s
into habitual goalscorers and, eventually, double winners, not to mention
one of the most exciting sides in English football. Bundling the ball – and
any opposing goalkeeper – into the back of the net was Smith's speciality,
though he had enough guile and wit to score 13 goals in 15 appearances
for England.

Tottenham Hotspur 2 v Leicester City 0

FA Cup Final
Saturday 6 May 1961

Wembley Stadium
Attendance 100,000

Spurs and Bobby Smith clinch the first double of the twentieth century

Teams

	Managers	
Bill Nicholson		Matt Gillies
Bill Brown	1	Gordon Banks
Peter Baker	2	Len Chalmers
Ron Henry	3	Richie Norman
Danny Blanchflower	4	Frank McLintock
Maurice Norman	5	Ian King
Dave Mackay	6	Colin Appleton
Cliff Jones	7	Howard Riley
John White	8	Jimmy Walsh
Bobby Smith	9	Hugh McIlmoyle
Les Allen	10	Ken Keyworth
Terry Dyson	11	Albert Cheesebrough

	Scorers	
Smith 66, Dyson 75		

Referee: J Kelly

THE TRUTH IS, I never should have played in the 1961 FA Cup final against Leciester – the game that clinched the record breaking double for Spurs. I shouldn't have even trained that week. I was injured, and wasn't really fit to play, but I was determined to be on that Wembley pitch. And the only way I could have played in that historic game was if I hid the truth from manager Bill Nicholson.

It was so nearly disastrous. The week before the Cup final I had busted my knee ligaments against West Bromwich Albion in the last League match of the season. I'd had the injury for a while and it was nag, nag, nagging me for months. Throughout the year it gradually got worse as the season went on, but I could handle it. Against West Brom I went in for a tackle and it flared up. We lost 2-1 – I'd scored our only goal, but I was in a lot of pain. I was terrified I was going to miss our last match of the season: the Cup final against Leicester. A game which would give us an opportunity to write our names forever into the history books.

My mood wasn't helped by the press reaction to the close of our League campaign. Even though we were Division One champions, we took a lot of flak after that defeat to West Brom because people said our mind was only on the Cup final. Certainly mine was. I'd always dreamt of it and I suddenly I had the very real fear of missing out through an injury.

I was a stubborn player and I usually gritted my teeth through pain on the park. The following day I had it in my mind that I wasn't going to miss the Cup final and I could battle my way through regardless, but it wasn't until I went into training on the Monday that I realised just how bad my knee was. I couldn't run on it. At times I couldn't even walk and I certainly couldn't kick a ball. So I knew I would have to have injections after the training sessions to mask the pain and the truth from Bill Nick.

I devised a plan. I went to the doctor on the quiet every morning that week. That way the coaching staff wouldn't get to know that I was in agony. Every day I'd get up and think, "I'm not going to miss this Cup final," and limp to the doctors for my jab. I was so close to my boyhood dream that I didn't want to blow it.

When I was a kid I thought about leaving football behind – I left my family in the northeast at 14 to join Chelsea and I didn't really want to go. I was only a boy. My dad said to me, "One day you'll regret it if you give up now. You might even get to a Cup final and you'll regret it if you don't keep going."

He was right. A Cup final is what you dream of when you're that age.

Then all of a sudden I'd got there with Tottenham and I'd got injured, putting my place and my dream in jeopardy. I couldn't believe it. So I went to the doctors and asked him if he had anything that could take the pain off. Every morning he'd give me a jab and I'd be alright for about four hours. I knew that if Bill Nicholson got the slightest indication I wasn't 100% fit then he wouldn't pick me. There were no squads or even substitutes in those days, so you couldn't risk a big player in case you picked up an injury straight away and had to play the rest of the game with ten men; especially not in a Cup final – and especially not in a Cup final that was going to win Spurs the double.

Anyway it came to the Friday before the game and I began to worry. I knew we were staying at Hendon Hall hotel before the game and so I wouldn't be nearby to the surgery. I called the doctor and he said, "Get to me in the morning and I'll put two jabs in for you, then you'll get through training in the morning, but don't go mad." I made sure I didn't do a lot of kicking in the training, so I didn't alert anyone.

It wasn't the training I was worried about though, it was the Cup final. I rang the doctor up that Friday evening, having survived training unscathed, and he asked me how I was.

"Beautiful," I said.

"Well, you're going to have to take two more jabs tomorrow if you're to get through. You'll have to come at nine in the morning, but you're going to need one at one o'clock if you're to get through the whole game."

Well, I knew that was going to be awkward – we had a sit down dinner planned at midday and it would be impossible to get away. The night before the game, Bill took us all to the pictures to see the film, *The Guns Of Navarone*. I think he wanted to take our minds off the game, but mine was on the injury. The next morning, I took my car to the hotel and I snuck out for the nine o'clock injection. Our trainer Cecil Poynton saw me and I said to him, "Don't say anthing to Bill. If he asks where I've gone at breakfast or something, just tell him I've gone for a walk." Cecil didn't know what was going on. I don't know what he must have thought when I climbed out of a side window to leave the hotel!

In truth, the only person who knew about the injury was Maurice Norman, my room mate. But apparently, when he woke up that Saturday morning, he looked across the room and saw my bed hadn't been slept in. He thought I'd spent the night on the town and was a little bit annoyed.

The truth was, I couldn't sleep at all – Maurice was snoring away – and dozed off in a chair in the corner of the room. Maurice was a true mate, though, and he ruffled my bed clothes in case Bill got suspicious. But I think Bill was a bit suspicious anyway. I think he knew I had a slight knock, but he had no idea just how bad it was. He knew I could play through a fair bit of pain though. He said to different people that I was the hardest git he'd seen go out there on a football pitch. Once I had a sceptic toenail during a game at Liverpool – it was sore, it had to come off. The doctor came up to me at half time and said, "I'll have to pull that off." I said, "Can't you leave it until after the game?" He said, "I can do," and gave me a jab. I gritted my teeth and got through the game. Cecil Poynton said afterwards, "If everybody had a heart as big as his we'd have a good time and a good team." Even back then, a number of players would get injured and make the most of it.

My attitude was: if you got dropped then somebody was going to take your place and I hated missing football matches. I rarely missed games. I played a lot of games I shouldn't have, but I enjoyed every minute of it, pain or no pain.

When I got to the doctors at one o'clock on Cup final day, he gave me the usual jabs and said, "These will keep you going until half time. When it gets to half time, you'll probably go as lame as a coot." He was right too. For the first half, I was involved in everything – running around, chasing loose balls, hassling defenders. Then, with about five minutes to go to the break, it started to kill me. I began to limp. At half time Bill Nick asked me what the matter was. I told him that I'd taken a knock in the game – I daren't tell him the truth. He told me to see the club doctor, who looked at my knee and said, "Here, have you been having any injections?"

I told him that I hadn't and thought of the only excuse that I could, which was that I'd been rubbing it since I'd picked up the supposed injury, which was why it looked a bit red and sore. I think he believed me – I got another couple of jabs and nobody was any the wiser.

Five minutes before full time it went again. Dave Mackay could see that I was struggling and told me not to move, just to stand around up front. I got through it and we won which was fantastic, because after a fabulous season we'd grabbed the double and made history.

Despite all that drama, the 1961 FA Cup final was a cracking game for me, regardless of the pain and the injections and the running around from doctor to training sessions. I scored one goal and set up the second for Terry Dyson – but that was actually the second chance of two that I had given him. Before his goal I'd turned a ball into him on the six yard box and he headed it over the top. For his goal I got to the wing, crossed the ball over and he put it in.

It was a joy just to be at Wembley, playing under the twin towers. It was a joy to play in front of all those Spurs fans. It felt like a once in the lifetime experience – something you had to make the most of – even though we got there the following year. I wasn't to know that and you never forget your first Cup final.

The pressure was on, though. We'd won the League and everyone else assumed that we would walk the final against relatively humble opposition in Leicester to win the double. People outside the club thought, "You've done the hard part, you've just got to go out there and win the Cup." But people inside the club knew it was a lot harder than that. Nobody else had done it that century, including Matt Busby's much vaunted Busby Babes, and one or two of our players were worried.

Captain Danny Blanchflower and Bill Nicholson were worried. You could see when we kicked off that some of the players weren't playing their usual game. You could tell that in the dressing room beforehand – the mood was quieter than usual. The stakes were high that day. On the pitch, the movement wasn't there. It is the classic Cup final problem: people were worried about making a mistake. No-one wanted to be the man that cost us the double.

Once we got the first goal we relaxed and started playing a little bit, but it wasn't a good game to watch. It was great because we'd won the double, but it wasn't one for the neutral. We made it harder for ourselves through all those nerves.

Instead we should have relaxed, gone out there and played our normal game. But I was determined to enjoy the day regardless of the mood. Before the game I stood in the tunnel – still in my suit, I hadn't got changed yet – so I could hear the band play *Abide With Me*. It was always one of my favourite hymns and I remember sneaking out to listen to it being played at Wembley, which used to happen amongst the communal singing in the half hour leading up to kick-off. It sounded fantastic.

Then Bill Nick came up to me and said, "Aren't you going to get ready?" I said "Oh I won't be long," and he looked at me sternly and said, "It's quarter to three!" The band finished playing the song and I raced back and got changed in ten minutes. Cecil started shouting at me: "Where the bloody hell have you been?" But I was prepared alright.

When you walked out onto the old Wembley pitch it was amazing. There was nowhere else in the world like it. The atmosphere was brilliant. All the people and the flags and the scarves, it was great. We walked out to this great reception and we were introduced to the Duchess of Kent. Apparently she turned round to Danny, who was introducing us all to her as they went along the line after the National Anthem, and said, "The Leicester players have their names on their tracksuits." And Danny replied with, "That's right, but we know each other." Which was typical of him. I remember she had tiny hands too and I didn't want to squeeze her too tightly.

It was even great playing on that Wembley pitch. It was a big surface, but it was very spongey, which a lot of players didn't realise. It killed the back of your legs and the ball bounced differently. I remember on the day before the game, we got to walk around the pitch and Bill got us all to take a ball with us, so we could get used to the feel of the grass. He was always very meticulous like that.

But the game was OK. I remember in the build up to the match that Leicester manager Matt Gillies had decided to drop their best player Ken Leek, but they still had a good team – Gordon Banks was in goal. But the game was short on excitement and Leicester were down to ten men for much of the game after Les Allen tackled one of their players, Len Chalmers. Len took quite a knock and had to go off. In those days there were no substitutes, so they were a man down. It meant they were forced to play very cautiously, which didn't make for a good spectacle. In fact I think the only exciting part of the game was when I scored my goal.

It's something you always dream about. For years and years – even when I was a just a little kid I used to think, "Wouldn't it be lovely to score in an FA Cup final?"

My dad always used to say to me, "If you get on in football, take your chances." He knew I'd do well if I got to Wembley. My parents are gone now, but everything he said to me came true. He said I could win an FA Cup and that I would do well. He always thought I would win the League with Spurs and I believed everything he said to me and they all came true. He guided me in those days. I admired my parents for that, my family always supported me. They came to watch the games and they got nervous for me. They came from Lindale near Redcar – a little mining village.

But I always did well at Wembley. I think I scored nearly every time I played there for England. But when I scored the goal against Leicester in that Cup final it was fantastic. I've still got photos of it. The ball came to me and I swivelled and hit it on the turn. I'm actually the only player to have scored two goals back to back in different FA Cup finals because we won the Cup the following year against Burnley and I scored the first goal that day. Even today I get kids and Spurs fans sending me pictures of that goal or of the double team lifting the FA Cup for me to sign for them. I love doing it. It's a fantastic memory, I sign them all and send them back.

If it wasn't for the fans I wouldn't be where I am today or talking about the great memories in football. But when I scored it was a fantastic feeling. It was like all my dreams come true. Even while I was celebrating the goal, I couldn't believe that I'd scored in a Cup final at Wembley. Your mind just goes wild. When you walk onto the pitch it's a fantastic experience, but you can't hear the crowd. When you're playing the game, you can't remember what's going on around you. Everything is done in the moment. It's only afterwards, when you stop to think about stuff, that it comes back to you and you can savour it. You realise that you really were there. It takes a long time for it to sink in.

I remember when I played for England against a Rest Of The World XI at Wembley, it was the same. We beat them 2-1. They had Puskas and a lot of wonderful players, but you don't realise what you've been doing until afterwards. So we won the Cup and the double and it was amazing. Once we knew that we'd won it felt like such an achievement. And it was an major acheivement in those days – you didn't have the squads that they have today. Remember, you weren't even allowed substitutions. We were the first to do it in the twentieth century and only Arsenal, Liverpool and Manchester United followed suit. Chelsea can't even manage it in the modern game! It was one of the proudest moments of my career.

Bill Nicholson didn't seem to be too excited. If I remember rightly, he was disappointed because we hadn't played particularly well. He was never one of those managers to say, "Oh well done," and get all excited about it. It was very reserved. He wouldn't go over the top. But I think he was very pleased that we did the double.

I was a very physical player at that time, I guess. In those days you could hit people with a shoulder barge or a hard tackle. You could barge goalkeepers and I think it was a better game for it – it was more physical in the box. The keepers never got the protection that they do today. But then goalkeepers could get away with murder too: they would go up and hit you with their elbow or they'd come down hard on you when they landed after catching a cross, so you had to defend yourselves.

Once they took that away from football, it ruined the English game. The fans loved it. And once people got used to it they enjoyed it. Yeah, some players were really dirty, and if they wanted to fight each other you'd get on with it. You'd give someone a dig and then that was it. But it was a better game than it is today. It's fast today, but it's false. You've got all these foreign players and they're ruining our game. I don't care what people say, they've ruined it. They're good footballers, don't get me wrong. Some of them are the best in the world. But they're always diving and holding their faces, waving imaginary cards. They've finished the English game. When the red cards and yellow cards came out, that was the end of it, everybody started trying to get other players in trouble.

At the end of the day, you want to be able to make tackles and challenge for the ball fairly, but hard. Players don't want to see the referee. They don't want to hear a whistle. If it's dirty, then the referee has to step in, but if it's hard but fair leave it alone.

I used to love going in on goalkeepers in the box and getting physical. I used to be very good friends with [Fulham and England captain] Johnny Haynes from our England days. Whenever Spurs used to play Fulham he would say to me, "Be careful with our keeper today."

Their keeper was terrified of me. I remember he was due to play for England a week after he played at our place. He said, "Alright Bobby. Please don't hit me against the post or anything like that." So I replied, "If you've got to go, you got to go." We used to laugh about it.

But this ball came up in the air and he was at the back post and I thought, "It's me or you mate." I went up for the header and smacked him into the post and the ball went into the net. We had some good times.

I played hard but fair. But I hated cheating. I remember we played one away game in the European Cup and the opposing goalkeeper spent most of the game spitting in my face. I hated it, it was disgusting. After the game he was sat near me when I was chatting to a local newspaper reporter. I told the journalist to translate to this player that when he got back to London he better pick up pneuomonia because he doesn't want to play at White Hart Lane – I was going to torment him for 90 minutes.

We kicked that game off and we had the centre all worked out. I touched it to Jimmy Greaves, he passed it back to Danny [Blanchflower] and he dropped it into their area at head height. All the time I was running towards the penalty box. This keeper could see the ball coming towards him and he could see me too. He didn't know what to focus on. I caught him with my shoulder and squashed him for our first goal. For the rest of the game he was scared. He spent more time watching me than the match. I loved it, I just prowled around winding him up. I got him a few times too. He was frightened to death in the end.

But we were physical all over the park. There was some brilliant players in that double winning side who had a lot of skill like Danny and Cliff [Jones], but there were a lot of tough players who didn't get the credit they deserved, like Terry Dyson, Les Allen – he was a great player, a lot of people didn't appreciate the hard work he put in – and Maurice Norman. It was like a jigsaw puzzle – we all fitted in. All the stars got the credit. But we were fantastic that season – I admired all those players, we all worked for each other. We were all in it together. That's why it was such a good side, because we all knew what the other players were going to do.

We were determined and competitive too. I remember our practice matches used to be really physcial because everyone wanted to win. We'd play XI-a-side. One team would have the forward line of the first team and some midfielders mixed in with reserves. The other team would have the first team defence and midfield with the reserve front line. It it would be bruising. Cliff Jones broke his leg in one of those game once. It was blood and thunder. And Bill was a good manager. He never interfered with you or what you were doing. Often when we went away for a game we used to go to the dogs the night beforehand, or people could do what they liked. As long as you got back on time and played well, he didn't care. He was sensible and so were we.

He was right to handle it in that way because we respected him. These days the players have to put up with so many rules and regulations – they can't do anything. We knew that if we had to play football on the Saturday, we weren't going to get drunk the night before. Bill Nick trusted us and we admired him for it.

The team spirit was great – we used to have arguments with each other in the dressing room, we even used to torment each other. But when we went on that pitch we looked out for each other. Dave Mackay used to say to Maurice Norman, "What's going to happen today, love? Are you going to be alright?" You know, really wind him up and tease him. But we enjoyed each other's company, especially on the pitch. It showed as well. That year we were brilliant – we won the League after winning the first 11 games of the season and were unbeaten for the first 16 games of the championship. I scored 28 league goals and five in the FA Cup too – I was Spurs' top scorer that year. The type of football Bill Nick loved to see us produce was so exciting to play in. It was push and run. Everybody was always moving.

In the end I was a bit disappointed in the way Spurs got rid of me. I was there ten years. We won the Cup in the year before I left. We got to the semis in the European Cup. We were a great team and I had scored a lot of goals for them, but they wouldn't give you any breathing space. If they decided your time was up, they'd get rid of you. I didn't want to leave Tottenham in 1963. I went to Brighton, but I wanted to stay at White Hart Lane. I was upset at the way they did it. At a club like Manchester United they never wanted to get rid of you if you'd done a good job for them. But Spurs wanted to buy Alan Gilzean and I had to go.

Saying that, I had a good year at Brighton. But I enjoyed every minute of my Spurs career. In fact I loved every minute of my football career and I remember when I gave it up, I didn't know what to do with myself. I was in a right pickle at first. It's such a big part of your life. You go to football training in the morning, you come back home in the afternoon and do what you like. After football I became a painter and decorator.

The memories I've got and the experiences I had I wouldn't swap it for the money they get today. Good luck to them, getting all that money, but when we played we were getting £16-£20 a week and I enjoyed every minute of it. Every second I was on the football pitch I was enjoying myself. When I got dropped I was unhappy. I didn't miss many games, mind. I played so many matches then Bill Nicholson would drop me to keep me sharp. He later admitted that he did it to make me have a think about my game.

I played 376 games for Tottenham and I scored 285 goals. I played 15 times for England and scored 13 goals – as I say, every time I played at Wembley I scored. It was a lovely place, a lovely stadium and I'm looking forward to going there when they open the new stadium.

Winning the FA Cup final and the double was the icing on the cake, even if we didn't play as well as we could. Thinking back I owe it all to that doctor. He got me on to the pitch for the final, one of the most amazing experiences of my life. Not only that, he got me an FA Cup winner's medal to go alongside the memories.

CLIFF JONES
WINGER 1958–1968

BORN   7 February 1935, Swansea
SIGNED   February 1958 from Swansea Town, £35,000
SPURS CAREER   370 games, 159 goals
HONOURS   Division One Champions 1961, FA Cup Winners 1961, 1962, 1967, European Cup Winner's Cup 1963, 59 full Welsh caps, 16 goals
LEFT   Transferred to Fulham, October 1968

The tricky winger with a fearless spirit and goal scoring instincts, Cliff Jones was signed by Spurs manager Bill Nicholson for a record breaking £35,000. He was an integral part of the Spurs side that won the double in 1961 and quickly became a coveted European star: Juventus even offered Tottenham a staggering £100,000 transfer fee, though they were unwilling to sell. "There was no braver player in the game than Cliff," said Nicholson, proudly, while fans and team-mates were equally in awe of his speed and wing play. "Spurs won't have any trouble when they want to get rid of you," quipped mid-fielder, Dave Mackay. "They'll just have to give you a ball, set you running, open up all the gates and you'll disappear up Tottenham High Road."

Tottenham Hotspur 8 v Gornik Zabrze 1

(Spurs win 10-5 on aggregate)

European Cup Qualifying Round second leg
Wednesday 20 September 1961

White Hart Lane
Attendance 57,737

Spurs announce themselves to the rest of Europe in style

Teams

Bill Nicholson	**Managers**	Augustyn Dziwisz
Bill Brown	1	Hubert Kostka
Peter Baker	2	Antoni Franosz
Ron Henry	3	Edward Olszowka
Danny Blanchflower	4	Ginter Gawlik
Maurice Norman	5	Stanislaw Oslizlo
Dave Mackay	6	Marian Olejnik
Cliff Jones	7	Stefan Florenski
John White	8	Erwin Wilczek
Bobby Smith	9	Edward Jankowski
Les Allen	10	Ernest Pohl
Terry Dyson	11	Roman Lentner
Blanchflower pen 10, Jones 20, 26, 36, Smith R 38, 71, Dyson 79, White 90	**Scorers**	Pohl 28

Referee: L Van Nuffell (Belgium)

I'LL NEVER FORGET IT. On that night we played better than any team who's ever played and whoever will play.

We attacked.

Goal.

We attacked.

Goal.

We attacked, attacked, attacked. Again, again, again.

Goal, goal, goal.

We were brilliant when we played Gornik Zabrze, I get goose bumps just thinking about it because it was such an incredible performance from a brilliant Spurs team. We swept right through them with such force, it was incredible. I don't think our opponents even knew what had hit them once the final whistle blew because we'd played so well. Nevertheless, it could have been so very different.

This was the second leg of two in a European Cup tie early in our first foray into Europe. We were going into the unknown, unlike today where European teams are on television every week. We had no idea what we were getting ourselves into. Spurs had qualified because we'd won the League during the previous season in 1961, the year of the famous double, but we had no previous experience in European competitions. In fact, this was the first European game at White Hart Lane so, as you can imagine, it was a particularly special occasion for everyone there.

Even so, the first game – the away leg – wasn't a very good match for us and could have ruined the White Hart Lane party. We hadn't played as well as we knew we could have done and Gornik Zabrze , to their credit, were a very good side. Still, it was a still surprise to us that we'd lost at the time – we were always confident of beating anybody. Having said that, Gornik featured most of the Polish national side in their team and had some out-standing players to call upon. They had quite an intimidating stadium, too. There was a 70,000 crowd for their home game and the atmosphere was fantastic. You could feel it once you got into the dressing room. So, all in all, it was a very difficult game for us. Looking back, we were lucky the score was only 4-2, which gave us a great chance to stay in the game, but only if we had a big result back at White Hart Lane a couple of weeks later.

As you can imagine, the following day we didn't get a very good write up in the press and Bill Nicholson wasn't very happy at all. The national reporters gave us a bit of a kicking, which was to be expected because we didn't play well in Poland and to some extent you have to accept the criticism that's thrown at you afterwards. At the same time, you had to give a lot of credit to Gornik Zabrze because they were a top side. So, we figured the result wasn't a complete disaster.

One or two other incidents had upset the press boys. Some of our players overstepped the mark a little bit in their tackling and Smithy [centre-forward, Bobby Smith] might have had one or two arguments with the opposition's centre halves, which he usually did. Bobby Smith would put himself about at corners and when he was going for headers, and people would whack him, but he'd take it. There was no whinging about it and after the game it was always forgotten about, but he'd always look after himself and give it back. I didn't condone it, but that's the way Bobby played and it was part of the game in those days. It was also very effective because opposition goalkeepers and defenders would be very wary when he began flying in for headers, which was something they weren't used to on the continent at that time. It was a good tactic for us.

Of course that didn't go down well with the Polish crowd during that first leg and it caused some ugly scenes. That, and the fact that we didn't play well or in our usual exciting style meant that the press got on to us and gave us some stick.

On reflection I can't say we underestimated Gornik at all. We tried to play our usual attacking football during that first leg, as we always did, but we were caught out on the break and paid the penalty. All of a sudden we were four goals down and really struggling, but we managed to claw a couple back. I scored one in that game and then Terry Dyson got the second. There weren't many Spurs fans there either, which was probably just as well – they wouldn't have had that much to cheer about, especially when the fourth went in early in the second half.

Bill wasn't happy at all at half-time with us two down. With Bill, winning wasn't enough. It had to be done in a certain style and with a certain level of quality. If we didn't reach that standard he wasn't happy – regardless of how we were doing result wise – so you can imagine what losing that badly meant to him. Later on in the season we beat Feyenoord

3-1 away from home in the European Cup in the first leg of the second round. You thought he'd be chuffed, but he wasn't happy. In fact, I remember when some reporters came into the dressing room, he shut the door for 15 minutes and gave us a bollocking. That was the thing with Bill: he had these standards and we had to attain them and we respected that.

As a manager, he knew what he was on about, though, because he worked hard on the game and knew more about football than any of us. He was great for Tottenham Hotspur – fans always talk about captain Danny Blanchflower, winger John White and Dave Mackay as the pivotal players in the team, but the main person was Bill Nicholson. He was in control. A top manager and a revolutionary one too.

For example, he would always say that the most important players in the team were the ones without the ball. The easiest thing in football, he'd say, is to get the ball because the other team will give it back to you eventually. However, the hard thing was to keep it and the only way to keep the ball was to always look to receive a pass and support the player with the ball. All our training was geared around possession and that was our trademark. We'd play keep ball in threes and twos – there were lots of different training techniques and it was very forward thinking.

Spurs were so ahead of their time that Bill even took us to see the Bolshoi Ballet. You can imagine what we thought: "Why are we going to the Bolshoi Ballet?" Anyway, we went and it was incredible. The experience was amazing. The ballet dancers were so fit and it impressed Bill so much that he had to find out how they trained. He went backstage and spoke to different choreographers and discovered the secret of their success: weight training. Anyway, from then on we had to train like ballet dancers. An Olympic weightlifter called Bill Watson came down to the ground with all these little weights and made us perform drills that were designed to give each player a little extra burst of power. You can laugh, but it really helped the way we performed – we were playing a totally different style of football to everyone else because we were so much quicker. Soon everyone was copying that idea.

Bill's other saying was, "You play the way you train. If you train with effort and method that's the way you'll play." His assistant coach Eddie Baily was always on hand to help out with practice – he had his own unique style which he brought to training and match days. Of course, as a former England forward himself, he reckoned he was much a better player than all of us, and he would tell us too. "You lot can't bloody play," he'd say. Now he's the only one left from the push'n'run side of the '50s. He was a top man. A typical cheeky chappy.

But that defeat in Poland conditioned Bill Nicholson – from then on he never went in to a first leg game in that attacking style, particularly away from home. He would bring in an extra defender and contain the opposition, knowing full well that if he kept the score down and they only scored one or two we could always pick it back up at Tottenham, and he was never going to let us get into a position where his team was four goals down. So he planned for our other games in meticulous detail. In that respect, the defeat at Gornik Zabrze was very important to Spurs because it affected the way in which he approached other European games.

But then, Bill was always renowned for doing his homework. If we were playing an away European match, he would head out there himself to see our opponents play. He'd also check out the accommodation where we were staying – which sometimes wasn't very nice compared to British standards. He would inform the hotel and often when we went back, things were changed to the way he wanted it.

Gornik was one of the worst towns I had ever been to, though. It was depressed. I felt really sorry for the people because it was a mining area and it wasn't particularly attractive. They obviously still suffered from the after effects of World War II and the communist regime which was in control at that time. But while it wasn't a particularly nice place to visit, the ground was completely different. It was an Olympic style stadium – the pitch, dressing rooms and running track were superb, as was so often the case in Eastern Europe. It stood out from the rest of the town.

That may have been our first European tie, but it wasn't the first time we'd played in Europe. At the end of the 1958/59 season Bill told us he was taking the team to Russia. I thought, 'You've got to be joking!' But we went to Russia for about two weeks. In a strange way it was a terrific bonding session for us. Bill had just signed Dave Mackay and he brought to the team all his commitment and influence. We played three or four games while we were over there. We didn't get beaten in any of them either, even though we were playing the brilliant Dynamo Kiev and a Russian Olympic XI – it really was the start of something big for us.

I had the unfortunate experience of having to share a room with Dave Mackay on those trips. I couldn't understand a word he was saying because he was Scottish and I was Welsh. It was so confusing, I even spoke to Bill about it.

"Can I have an interpreter?" I asked.

"What for, the Russian?"

"No, a Scottish one. I can't understand a word Mackay's saying to me."

But Dave was a terrific friend and a player. What you saw on the pitch was what he was like all the time: committed. He was probably the best player I'd ever worked with and he was a great influence on the side. But I played with some great footballers in that Tottenham team – John White, our other winger, was one of the greatest players ever and would terrify defences when he was running at them.

So Russia was a great learning experience. It felt like a bit of an adventure. It was something very different for us and certainly European football was something we'd never experienced before, but it really built us as a team.

Bill had us motivated for the second leg against Gornik Zabrze at White Hart Lane. In practice sessions he got us all fired up. Before the game he would get the training to a really intense level and in his team meetings he stressed that, right from the off, we had to get at the Gornik Zabrze team and play them off the park.

On the night of the game we were so expectant, but so were the crowd when we came out for kick-off. This always stands out in my mind – I remember jogging out of the tunnel, which was in the far corner of the ground at that time, towards the East Stand and a roar hit me. The noise was like a wall. It was incredible and that sound will always stay with me, because I have never known an atmosphere in all my life like it. I've played at Hampden Park and Ninian Park, Wembley, the Maracana... but nothing matched the atmosphere at White Hart Lane that night. When they talk about the atmosphere of the Glory, Glory Days, that was it right there.

We had great fans, and I have so much respect for them. In those days the players were much more attached to the supporters and after the game we would go to the Bell and Hare pub by the ground and have a couple of pints. There was nothing wrong with that and we would have a chat with the fans – it was good for the players, good for the supporters and good for the club.

These days, that doesn't happen and the supporter doesn't get near the player, which is a shame. In that era, the fans could identify with the players and in many ways, they were no different from us. I guess you could say we got paid a bit more money than the man in the street, but still our lifestyles were very similar. I even lived in the local area, Bobby Smith a few doors away from me. It was a totally different era. These days they've got houses in Saudi. I reckon it was much better in those days – the supporter was an important part of the team.

Because this was the first European game at White Hart Lane, it was something very very special, for the team, for the fans and for the football club. There were over 57,000 people crammed into the ground and in those days there was very little seating at White Hart Lane, so the crowd were extremely close to the playing area. White Hart Lane was totally different to what it is today – there was no running track – and the crowd were right on top of you when you played. It had a brilliant effect: you could see in the Gornik Zabrze players straight away that they were intimidated by it. It felt like we'd gone a goal up before we'd even kicked a ball. We weren't expecting it and it certainly shocked the Gornik Zabrze team. It lifted us, but it knocked them right down. The fans just picked us up and chucked us at 'em and we just slaughtered Gornik Zabrze from the off.

It was an unforgettable 90 minutes. Right from the start we went on the attack and swept them aside. Danny [Blanchflower] scored in the first minute with a penalty, which was a relief because Bill knew we had to rattle them with an early goal. That's what the crowd were looking for and straightaway we turned to each other and thought, "Here we go". Our attitude was 'Let's get at them'. I don't think they ever matched us from that moment.

We had such a pace to our game that night. We played quick, push and run football, where you would play the ball to a team-mate and then run into space. Of course, Bill had brought that in from his time playing for the very famous [former Spurs manager] Arthur Rowe in the '50s. That was the way he was taught to play and he developed it further, playing with a bit more pace here and a bit of extra power there. Bill's team also had individuals like myself and John White who would dribble with the ball, but we were never allowed to dribble too much. Bill was always on at me when I had the ball at my feet: "Pass the bloody thing, Cliff!"

Of course, our game-winning, individual players and the team ethic all came together that night. We were 1-0 up and then I scored what you could call the perfect hat-trick – a header, a goal with my right foot and another with my left. It was complete and they all came one after the other. After Danny's penalty, I scored a header to pull us back to four all and from that moment we really believed we were going to win. That goal was a good one, too. The cross came over from Terry Dyson on the left and I got up and met it well. Heading goals was one of my trademarks – I was always on the look out for them. I felt that I always had an advantage because I had a knack of always seeing the ball as it came across and the defender at the same time from my wing position, so as long as I timed my run well and as long as I was brave enough, I'd get to it, which I did a number of times.

Straightaway I got another – my second goal and our third. The ball came out to me and I just hit it instinctively with my right foot. When we were playing attacking football, like we were on that night, it was very easy to perform well because we had John White and he was a great footballer, so quick and so skilful. What had attracted Bill to sign John White was that he was doing national service and he was the Army's cross country champion. Now, Bill loved players who'd get about the pitch and John was perfect for him. We needed someone who could link up the play on the park between attack and defence and John was brilliant at it. They called him 'The Ghost' because he would float around the pitch and he was so difficult to mark. Players found it impossible, especially that night. We always knew that when we picked up the ball there'd be at least one pass on: John White.

So we were ahead, but then their inside-forward scored probably one of the best goals I'd ever seen. It was a right foot volley that he hit from about 25 yards out. It went straight past keeper Bill Brown – which wasn't an easy thing to do, because he was a very good keeper – to bring them level again. I suppose you could compare it to a Wayne Rooney volley, although the ball was a bit different in those days wasn't it? If you could hit it 25 yards like that you must have had some shot on you.

Anyway, it was now 5-5 on aggregate, but we knew we had them beaten. It didn't take the wind out of our sails at all. There was only going to be one result. Right from the start, once the referee blew his whistle, we knew there was only going to be one winner. We just swept them aside from the restart and luckily I came straight back at them and got one with my left, before Terry Dyson and Bobby Smith got a couple to put us through.

Bobby was a great striker, particularly in Europe. European opponents had never experienced his style of play. On the continent goalkeepers were allowed to catch the ball, bounce it and clear it upfield without any hassle. That never happened when Bobby was around. They got bounced and, of course, keepers didn't like it. Bobby would go up with the defenders and he would frighten them, so in some ways he was one of our most effective players. It would affect their game and we would cash in on it because we'd put balls into the box and the keeper would have one eye on the ball and another on what Bobby was doing – normally looking to clatter him. It was a recipe for success.

That reputation spread throughout Europe and I know that when the draws were made, the other clubs didn't want to meet us. They knew we could play football to match the top football sides, but we could mix it as well. We were physical. When you're looking for a top side, we were it because we had it all.

But we were a good side right the way through the team, that's why we did so well. We had Bill Brown in goal who was a great shot stopper. He wasn't an enormous character like somebody like Pat Jennings, so he would take a few knocks coming off his line, but his shot stopping was great. He was a very calm personality – he was the only Scotsman I could understand!

The back four was very strong – we had Maurice Norman, who was a great centre half, Peter Baker and Ron Henry were very underrated and then you had Blanchflower, who was just great for the team because he bridged the gap between the boardroom and the dressing room. He could talk at any level – to kids, players, fans, directors – but he did go on a bit at team talks. Bill would ask if anyone of us had questions at the end of our meetings and Danny would always stand up.

"Just one thing, Bill".

We would think, "Oh no." And he would go on, and on, talking for hours. We wouldn't know what he was talking about either. He would say "I'm just going to finish on this now." And then he'd go on for another thirty minutes. He could talk for an hour on pretty much anything – if he actually knew something about it, two hours. But when Danny was on the field, he made sure Bill's instructions were carried out to the letter, which you don't see these days because the coaches on the sideline call the shots. In that team Danny would do it, because he had the intelligence and he was a terrific player.

That team was a great blend of players and it all worked out against Gornik, but that was down to Bill Nicholson. He brought us all together, and this was even before Jimmy Greaves arrived later that season. He was the best goalscorer I'd ever seen, without a doubt. I always felt sorry for Les Allen because, although we did the double and he got 27 goals, he had to make way for Jimmy.

Strangely, we were a better side the year after the double and we should have done the double in '62 too – in fact that year we were the first team in England to chase the treble. We won the FA Cup and were unlucky not to win the League again. I remember eventual Champions Ipswich beat us during the season twice, which cost us the title really. When we played them in the Charity Shield the following season we hammered them 5-1. We were a different class of side to them and we should have beaten them at least once that year.

And we should have won the European Cup too. We overcame Feyenoord 4-2 on aggregate before beating Dukla Prague in the quarter-finals. I see Jimmy Greaves today and he is still adamant that we were cheated out of winning the European Cup semi-final against Benfica because we had three goals disallowed by the ref and went out 4-3 on aggregate. We didn't have the rub of the green that's for sure. But there were some fantastic teams in Europe at that time.

I get goose bumps just thinking about playing in the European Cup. I have lots of memories about games, but that increible night against Gornik Zabrze was the one that always sticks in my mind. Even more so than the cup finals. That game was an Experience. European football was a glamorous novelty for everyone and we had the all white strip on as well. We all loved the all white strip, especially when the floodlights were on and when you played in the evening, in the cold, the air seemed a lot sharper somehow. It was an incredible experience. Winning the double, winning the European Cup Winners Cup in 1963, beating Leicester in the FA Cup Final were all great moments, but that night at White Hart Lane was something else.

After the game, Bill was delighted, there was no doubt about it. He knew it was a sensational performance and he was pleased. But Bill would never show too much emotion – I think he was afraid that we might become overly complacent if he gave us too much credit. He would always tell you quietly if you did well, but you could never really believe it when you heard it. After that game, after scoring a hat-trick, he came up to me and said "Well done, son"

I couldn't believe it. "A pat on the back, Bill, what have I done to deserve this?" And he looked at me and said, "A pat on the back is only a couple of feet away from a kick up the arse."

We never used to mix with the opposition after the games. In the First Division, if we were playing away we'd have to get the 5.30 train back to London, so there was never any time for a pint with the other teams. There certainly wasn't any time for ice baths and nutritional shakes or whatever it is they have today. And that was a shame.

In rugby that social behaviour was encouraged, but we never did that in football. There was little communication on the pitch between us and Gornik either – which was why any trouble between the teams always carried over into two legs. I remember Bobby Smith getting hold of a player who'd been kicking him during a European tie and telling him, "Londres, Londres." I think he meant he'd get him back in the return leg in London.

I was saying "Londres? Bobby what are you on about?" There was never any shirt swapping going on in those days either. Bill wouldn't have been happy if we had. We only had a limited number of kits.

Football was harder in those days too – there were no substitutes, the seasons were longer, there were more games and the conditions and pitches were terrible. If you look at White Hart Lane now, the pitch is incredible – a brilliant playing surface. In those days it was a mess. I wouldn't have a problem playing in football today, but I don't think the players of the modern generation could adjust to our style of play. The equipment was so much different in those days, particularly the ball. How would today's players cope with that?

Still, I wouldn't change the era that I played in for a second. It was the Glory Days, it was the swinging sixties, it was just great. I wouldn't change one little thing about it. I have realised over the years that you have to live for today, but there's nothing wrong with enjoying your memories.

DAVE MACKAY
MIDFIELD 1959–1968

BORN   14 November 1934, Edinburgh
SIGNED   March 1959 from Hearts; £32,000
SPURS CAREER   318 appearances, 51 goals
HONOURS   Division One Champions 1961; FA Cup Winners 1961, 1962, 1967; European Cup Winner's Cup 1963, 22 full Scotland caps
LEFT   Transferred to Derby County, July 1968; £5,000

The legendary Spurs captain of the 1960s, hardman Dave Mackay was an inspirational figure on and off the field with an insatiable desire for work and prodigious will to win; in 40 cup finals at all levels, he never finished on the losing side. Blessed with superb ball control, a sweet strike and sublime distribution skills, Mackay was a member of Spurs' 1960/61 double team and FA Cup winning side 12 months later. Recovering from a twice-broken left leg, Mackay captained Tottenham to a third FA Cup triumph of the sixties in 1967, before joining Derby County, where he became joint Footballer of the Year. in 1968/69. As County manager, he won the First Division title in 1974/75. Prior to joining Spurs, Mackay won every domestic honour with his hometown club Hearts, including the League title in 1957/58 and he appeared for Scotland in the 1958 World Cup finals.

Tottenham Hotspur 3 v Burnley 1

FA Cup Final
Saturday 5 May 1962

Wembley Stadium
Attendance 100,000

Spurs become only the second team to retain the FA Cup in the twentieth century – and almost complete a double Double

Teams

Bill Nicholson	**Managers**	Harry Potts
Bill Brown	1	Adam Blacklaw
Peter Baker	2	John Angus
Ron Henry	3	Alex Elder
Danny Blanchflower	4	Jimmy Adamson
Maurice Norman	5	Tommy Cummings
Dave Mackay	6	Brian Miller
Terry Medwin	7	John Connelly
John White	8	Jimmy McIlroy
Bobby Smith	9	Ray Pointer
Jimmy Greaves	10	Jimmy Robson
Cliff Jones	11	Gordon Harris
Greaves 3, Smith 51, Blanchflower (pen) 80	**Scorers**	Robson 50

Referee: J Finney

TOTTENHAM HOTSPUR in the 1960s was a wonderful place to be a professional footballer. We had great players, played with plenty of style and entertained supporters up and down the country. I also played against some of the greatest players to grace the game and, of course, we set a standard for other clubs to chase when we won the double in 1960/61. It was a tremendous achievement, but what is forgotten nowadays is how close we came to winning the double again the following season. No team has ever won back-to-back FA Cup and League doubles, but we came so close to achieving that in the middle of a golden era at White Hart Lane.

Growing up in Edinburgh, football was a major part of my life. Only a couple of years separated my elder brother Tommy, younger brother Frank and me. Another brother, Ronnie, was born after my dad came home from the war. Like lots of boys from our era, Tommy, Frank and I just had a tennis ball to practice with and did so at every opportunity. We didn't walk or run to school, we dribbled the ball to school along the pavement.

For as long as I can remember, I wanted to be a professional footballer. I would have joined any club to get my opportunity, but my number one choice was Hearts. All the family followed Hearts' fortunes every week and, from the age of eight, I stood on the terraces opposite the main stand at Tynecastle with Tommy and Frank.

The three of us were centre-halves for a local club called Saughton Park and it was a big story one year in local newspapers because the teacher in charge would not play us together in the Scottish Schoolboy's Cup as he wasn't sure that we had a chance. The following year we faced Kings Park in the final at Hampden Park and he did play us. It was every schoolboy's dream to play at Hampden and a marvellous moment for our family. All schools competed for the cup, as it was the most prestigious schoolboy trophy. We drew 0-0, which was incredible as many games could finish 5-0, 6-5 even 10-0. We thought the replay may be at Hibernian's Easter Road ground, but for the three of us the perfect venue was Hearts' ground, Tynecastle. Incredibly, we got our wish and Tommy scored in a 2-1 win. It was a fantastic occasion.

In April 1952, when I was 17, Hibs manager Hugh Shaw arranged to see me. But Hearts groundsman Mattie Chalmers lived four doors from us and I'm sure my dad went to speak to him, because manager Tommy Walker asked me to come down to the club. I went to Tynecastle the day before I was due to see Hibs. I wanted to sign for Hearts more than any other team and got my wish. Tommy, who played semi-professional for Edinburgh City, and Frank later signed for Hearts, but neither made the first team.

Hearts loaned me to Newton Grange Star Juniors to begin with, where I played wing-half in an open age League. We played the W-M formation, two full backs, a centre-back, two wing halves and five forwards. The back three were all over 30 years of age. I was one of two youngsters that did all the running for the older players. We had a great time and won five trophies. Hearts gave us an engraved watch to mark the achievement.

Hearts had not won a trophy for 49 years when I made my debut against Clyde in November 1953, but we quickly developed and picked up four major honours during my years at the club. Alfie Conn, Jimmy Wardhaugh and Willie Bauld were dubbed the 'terrible trio' as they did the damage in attack. In fact, they scored so many goals we used to paralyse teams. Historically, Rangers and Celtic won the League every year. Hibernian and Aberdeen broke the domination ocasionally, so for Hearts fans it was fantastic to come from nowhere and challenge for major honours.

The breakthrough came in the Scottish League Cup when we defeated Motherwell 4-2 in the 1955 final, Willie Bauld getting a hat-trick. Then the following season we beat Celtic 3-1 to win the Scottish Cup. We let one goal in during the run against Forfar Athletic, Stirling Albion, Rangers and Raith Rovers before Ian Crawford with two and Alfie Conn settled the final.

I was appointed captain for the 1956/57 campaign, which was a huge honour and we finished runners-up to Rangers by two points. This was the second time we'd finished second, as Celtic edged the title in my first season at Hearts. In 1957/58, we made no mistake and won the First Division championship, finishing 13 points clear of Rangers. To lift the champion's flag was a very special moment. The season was also memorable because, having played for Scotland Schoolboys, I won my first full cap for Scotland against Spain and played in the World Cup finals.

The team did not have a manager in Sweden, but on our return, Matt Busby was appointed and took charge when Scotland played Wales in Cardiff at the start of the new campaign. We trained at Reading's ground before travelling. Matt took me aside and said, "Davie, you take throw-ins, free kicks and penalty kicks. How do you take penalties?" We tried a few; it was only practice so you could hardly miss. Matt said, "I don't like penalties being taken with the side of the foot because if a keeper guesses the right way he'll save it unless its six inches from the post." I thought, "no problem," and battered a few straight in.

Come the match, in the opening minute, Mel Hopkins brings down Bobby Collins for a penalty. As Matt requested, I stepped up and whacked the ball as hard as I could. Jack Kelsey saved it. It was a bad penalty. Matt apologised after, but thankfully it didn't matter because we won 3-0. Some years later I was talking to one our players from that day and he'd forgotten I'd missed, but only because we won. If we had drawn or lost, you can be sure he'd have remembered! Matt didn't last long as manager as he was rebuilding Manchester United after the Munich air disaster.

Every time that I played for Scotland, it was brilliant, though I wasn't selected as often as I'd have liked due to injuries. We had some great Scottish players playing in Scotland but the strength in depth of Scottish players in England was far greater. Bill Shankly took Denis Law, Don Revie took Billy Bremner and many other great players made their names in England. It always puzzled me that they were not picked up first by a Scottish club.

In what would be my last season with Hearts I picked up another League Cup winner's medal when we defeated Partick Thistle 5-1 in 1959, Willie Bauld and Jimmy Murray grabbing two apiece. What pleased me about my Hearts career was that we competed at the highest level and finished in the top-four every season.

I was a combative player and always went in for hard tackles. This cost me during my time at Tynecastle because I broke my foot three times. When Tottenham Hotspur offered £32,000 before the transfer deadline in March 1959, Hearts accepted, deciding that if I got another bad injury I may be finished. Tommy Walker said I could think it over, but there was nothing to think over. My transfer from Hearts to Tottenham was a then British record for a wing-half.

I have always been lucky, and looking back, the move was at the right time. Tottenham, under manager Arthur Rowe, had won the First Division title in the early 50s, but after slipping down the league and climbing back into the top-three had slipped back again. Bill Nicholson had replaced Jimmy Adamson as manager. Spurs were leaking goals and Bill Nick believed I could help them become tighter in defence and score goals. He was also confident I could fit in alongside the likes of Tommy Harmer, Danny Blachflower, Maurice Norman and Bobby Smith.

When I first met Bill Nick in Edinburgh to discuss a move, I realised quickly that I wanted to sign for him. His team had just defeated Everton 10-4, which was a fantastic result, but they went through a terrible run. Tottenham were just above the relegation zone when we defeated Manchester City 3-1 on my debut. A 5-0 win over West Brom in our final home game saw us safe.

My dream as a kid, other than playing at Hampden Park, was to play at Wembley Stadium because I had never seen such a pitch in my life. Watching the FA Cup final on television every year in Scotland, it looked unbelievable, whereas Hampden Park was a wee bit lumpy and jumpy. I soon found out for myself because I represented Scotland Schoolboys against England Schoolboys at Wembley in 1950. Johnny Haynes was in the England side and I came up against Johnny in a full international a few weeks after I joined Tottenham. England edged a 1-0 win and Billy Wright won his 100th cap. Johnny broke a finger following a heavy challenge by me. Wembley was everything I imagined, but I was desperate to play in a Cup Final there.

By New Year 1961, the double side-to-be was in place, with Bill Brown, Ron Henry, John White and Les Allen cementing first team spots. There were plenty of jokers in the dressing room, especially Bobby Smith, Terry Dyson and myself. Danny Blanchflower was the governor type and there was great camaraderie. After an early game, Terry said to me, "Davie, do you want to go for a drink?" I said, "I'll follow you in the car," but he explained that they drank around the corner at the Bell and Hare. At Hearts, you could not drink within a couple of miles of the ground after the game! Bill Nick didn't like us drinking, but we didn't have a game for a few days, so felt it was OK and it was great having a room to relax.

Whatever Bill Nick said was always nice and sensible. On a Friday, after four days hard training you could do whatever you wanted to do as long as you had a 15-minute five-a-side game in the gym. I had never experienced this. If you wanted to go out on the track that was OK, there would be nobody there demanding, "do five laps, three laps or two strong laps then sprints." Depending on how I felt, I'd do different things, which was fantastic.

Growing up in Scotland, every year we watched the FA Cup final. The first one I saw was the 'Matthews Final' in 1953 when Blackpool defeated Bolton Wanderers. I used to love wingers like Stan, Tom Finney and later

Jimmy Johnstone of Celtic and Tommy Henderson of Rangers. They were all fantastic footballers.

Bill Nick's only selection decision in that team was whether to select Cliff Jones or Terry Medwin on the right wing. You never knew which way Cliff was going to go as he could play on either wing, but operated on the left during the 1960/61 campaign. Cliff was fast, tricky and brave. Often he'd make a late run to finish off a move with a neat header or strike.

Like Cliff, Terry played on both wings and also played occasionally at centre-forward. He was strong in the air and a very dangerous player. Bill Nick chose Cliff at the start of the campaign and he remained first choice apart from injuries.

On the left wing was Terry Dyson; he was some player. Terry was just over five foot tall, but caused problems for opponents with his skill and would score crucial goals during the coming season. I was disappointed when out-and-out wingers disappeared from the game. I loved having wingers in my team because, other than scoring goals, they offered the most entertainment you can get in football. There was no finer sight than a winger taking on an opponent; guys like Tom Finney and Stan Matthews were entertainment on their own.

At inside-forward were John White and Les Allen. John was slight, but gave us balance, had a great strike and was extremely dangerous because he used to drift in from the left flank in the main. Tragically, he was stuck by lightning during the summer of 1964 while sheltering under an oak tree during a round of golf with Cliff and died. He was such a popular guy, it was dreadful. Les was much stronger and an excellent player. Hard working, instinctive in the penalty area and unselfish, Les scored important goals for Tottenham.

Bobby Smith was a terrific leader of the line and a prolific goalscorer. I didn't mind playing against anyone, but one guy I would not have liked to face was Bobby because he was big, strong, powerful and awkward to mark. Bobby was excellent in the air, bustled past opponents and was a nightmare for goalkeepers at set-pieces.

I was confident we would make an impact during the season and was right because we made an excellent start to the 1960/61 campaign, winning our opening 11 league games. We began with an opening day 2-0 win against Everton and among our victories were four-goal triumphs over Blackburn Rovers and Manchester United, and a 6-2 thumping against Aston Villa, a match in which I scored my opening goal of the season.

Everything just clicked and we made it go right because the team knitted so well. We had only just started together but it worked out, which was fantastic and you must give credit to Bill Nick for changing what was a bottom-four team. Our initial target in 1959 was let's escape relegation because that's where we were at that particular time. Now the target was to win a trophy.

Five consecutive wins in December, including a fine 3-1 win at rivals Everton when I scored our opening goal, meant we had won 22 out of 25 league games, which was incredible. We had a points cushion and talk now was of the double with the FA Cup coming up. We felt confident but realised a lot of football had to be played.

I loved the competition and atmosphere of a big cup-tie because it was a one-off so both teams had a chance on the day. It was that bit different for not only players, but also supporters and with us going so well in the League there was that extra feeling of anticipation at the club. The 1961 FA Cup run went relatively smoothly for us and with Leicester suffering an injury in the Final, we won that game comfortably too, to add to the league title which we'd clinched with a 12 point margin.

At the final whistle, I was so happy. We all congratulated each other and really tried to take in the atmosphere. Suddenly, it was time for Danny to collect the trophy, before we posed for photographs and enjoyed the lap of honour. Bill Nick waited for us to shake us all by the hand before the celebrations continued in the dressing room where there was lots of signing.

We'd claimed the double, which is much more than just winning the FA Cup. Achieving the double was important but I realised it would not sink in for some time. However, we were in cloud cuckoo land, away up with the fairies. After a celebratory dinner at the Savoy the following day, we went on an open top bus to show off the trophy to supporters.

During the summer, I played plenty of golf and attended a number of functions. Up until 1961, we were earning £20 a week. This was the first season without the maximum wage and you were lucky if you could negotiate more then £100 a week. Spurs were now in the European Cup, so had an exciting season ahead of us. We knew that we would be the team to beat, but went into the campaign thinking we could win the double again.

Our title defence began slowly compared to the previous season as we collected just five wins in the opening 10 games. I was in and out of the side due to injury, but managed a goal in a 1-0 win at home to Wolves. As we settled into the title race alongside Burnley and newly promoted Ipswich

Town, managed by former Tottenham player Alf Ramsey, we played in the European Cup for the first time. It was brilliant to take part against the best European sides, but we did struggle to win games immediately after a midweek away fixture.

We advanced into the quarter-finals, following aggregate wins over Gornik Zabrze and Feyenoord, but picked up only one League victory after the four ties and if you are not winning games after a European match, you will struggle to win the League. Without making excuses, playing in, say, Poland was not straightforward like it is today, with direct flights and motorway systems. We would play Wednesday, travel back Thursday then quite probably be off again on Friday for a domestic away match. We were also not eating as well, but I would not have missed the European adventure.

In early December, Bill Nick strengthened our side with the purchase of Jimmy Greaves. A prolific scorer of goals, I had faced Jimmy in his Chelsea days and he was a terrific goalscorer. After a spell in Italy with AC Milan, Jimmy joined Tottenham for just under £100,000, a huge amount of money in the early 60s. With Bobby Smith sidelined, Jimmy came straight into the side and would prove a great addition to the team.

I was still troubled with an injury as was Terry Dyson, who was replaced by Terry Medwin. I came back into the first team and scored in a 3-1 win over Birmingham City before Jimmy marked his debut with a hat-trick in a 5-2 win over Blackpool. Over the festive period, we enjoyed a double over Chelsea to send us into the New Year challenging for the title.

Our defence of the FA Cup was now upon us and we fancied our chances of doing well. There was a real sense that we had an opportunity of defending the Cup, but, naturally, we had to take each match as it came. As usual, we listened out for the draw on the radio after training and the third round could have been kinder as we faced a trip to fellow First Division side Birmingham City.

The match proved far more difficult than we anticipated [Birmingham were fighting relegation at the time] and we had to dig deep to come from three goals behind to force a 3-3 draw. I remember that it was a windy day and the game was over by half-time, or so we thought, but as the wind advantage switched, Jimmy Greaves and Terry Dyson earned us an unlikely replay, which we won 4-2 in front of a packed house at White Hart Lane. Terry Medwin grabbed two goals.

We had a comfortable win in round four at lower league opposition. Facing Plymouth Argyle, we realised that the first game was their best opportunity of causing an upset, but the result was never really in doubt, as we ran out 5-1 winners. Jimmy scored two goals and was really beginning to make his mark with Tottenham supporters.

Before our fifth round clash at West Brom, we returned to European Cup action with a trip to Dukla Prague. It was a tiring journey, but we returned with a chance of progressing to the semi-finals following a narrow 1-0 defeat. We'd struggled on our return from European legs to date but made no mistake this time with a 4-2 victory at The Hawthorns. Bobby Smith was back in the side for Les Allen, which could not have been an easy decision for Bill Nick, but Bobby and Jimmy Greaves leading the attack was some prospect. Bobby struck twice, as did Jimmy; one goal in particular being one of Jimmy's special goals.

Greavesie was without doubt the most natural goalscorer that I played with during my football career. Jimmy had tremendous balance, anticipation in the penalty area and finished clinically. We knew that when Jimmy was one on one with a goalkeeper it was a goal. Other players, if they were through on a keeper six times would maybe score four. Jimmy would score all the time. If we were under pressure, often the ball would be knocked up to Jimmy 40 yards out; he'd take the defence on and score a great goal.

Although a great goalscorer, he was not a great trainer. During pre-season, Jimmy wouldn't come in from a road run until I'd be back and showered. He just couldn't do it... but come Saturday, he was one of the best players and every time you saw a picture of the six-yard box Jimmy was always there; he was match sharp.

It was great to be in the FA Cup quarter-finals, but there was no time to celebrate as we faced the return leg with Dukla Prague at White Hart Lane. I grabbed two goals in a terrific 4-1 win to set up a semi-final clash with Benfica, who had great players including Portuguese legend Eusebio. The matches were now coming thick and fast. Although I'd been ever-present in both cup competitions, I had missed a number of League games and all the big matches had affected our title defence. Since our Boxing Day win over Chelsea, we'd picked up just two victories, which allowed Burnley and Ipswich to build up a decisive-looking points advantage that we would struggle to claw back.

There was no time to feel sorry for ourselves though. We had to battle on and now faced Aston Villa in the Cup. At least we had a home draw and made it count in a 2-0 win; Danny Blanchflower and Cliff Jones grabbed the goals. Reaching the semi-finals gave us just the boost we needed before we travelled to Benfica and played vital League games. Against the Portuguese champions, we lost 3-1 at the Stadium of Light, but felt aggrieved as we had two goals disallowed that appeared fine. Bobby Smith's goal however kept us in the game.

Back in the League, I missed a 3-1 win over Everton that kept us in the title hunt, but was fit for a glamour clash with Manchester United in the FA Cup semi-finals. Burnley played Fulham in the other semi-final, but our match was the one that generated massive interest. Playing United was always a special occasion as they had fanatical support and with players like Bobby Charlton in the team would be always dangerous. The match was played in an intense atmosphere and we played really well to win 3-1. Terry Medwin, Jimmy Greaves and Cliff Jones scored. Our dressing room was really buzzing with the prospect of playing either Burnley or Fulham in the final following their draw.

To defend the FA Cup was no mean feat. Only Newcastle United had achieved it at Wembley since the stadium's construction in 1923, so it was a huge target for us. Reaching the final could not have been better preparation for the return clash with Benfica, but we bowed out of the European Cup on aggregate 4-3, after winning 2-0 at White Hart Lane. We were unfortunate, though, because I hit the bar in the last minute. Had it gone in we'd have gone to extra time. Benfica's coach said that whoever won the semi-final would win the final and that proved to be true as Benfica defeated Real Madrid 5-3 in Amsterdam. Eusebio said I was the best wing-half in the world he'd faced, which was some accolade.

I missed the next few matches as our League campaign faltered again. Despite winning four of our five remaining games, we finished behind Ipswich, who edged out Burnley after they slipped badly in the run-in. I scored in the final two games as we defeated Birmingham and Leicester City 3-2, but Ipswich finished four points ahead of us. Throughout the season few sports writers had given newly promoted Ipswich a chance of lasting the distance, but with Ray Crawford and Ted Phillips leading the line they scored plenty of goals. Our away form had cost us, but we had come close to retaining our league title. If we'd not lost at home against Ipswich 3-1 between the FA Cup fifth and sixth rounds we'd have retained it on goal average. It was that tight.

It wasn't strange being back at Wembley, we expected to be and looked forward to facing Burnley after they won their semi-final replay against Fulham. As always, we fancied our chances. All the team felt we were the best side around. Burnley was a team under pressure as they'd let the League slip from their grasp, whereas we'd been through the pressure of a Cup final before and appeared more relaxed in the days leading to the game.

Come the big day, we didn't have any injury concerns. Since the fifth round, we'd played the same XI, so the team picked itself. The only changes from the Leicester final saw Terry Medwin and Jimmy Greaves line up instead of Terry Dyson and Les Allen. Our preparation was similar to the previous year and we knew what to expect. Bill Nick gave his last instructions before we got the call to line up in the tunnel. Tottenham supporters were in fine voice and the walk out was special before we met the dignitaries that included the Queen, Duke of Edinburgh and Duke of Gloucester.

Determined to play well, we made the perfect start and caught Burnley by surprise with a goal inside three minutes. Bobby Smith created the opening for Jimmy Greaves from Bill Brown's long ball upfield. Jimmy didn't control the ball perfectly, but still had enough composure to beat Tommy Cummings and slide the ball home past keeper Adam Blacklaw.

Burnley had to come at us and did carve out openings, but their finishing was not clinical. If Jimmy had been in their attack, we'd have been in trouble. They did go close, though, and Bill Brown had to be alert to turn a Brian Miller strike over the bar. Jimmy nearly doubled our lead on 19 minutes when he burst through past Cummings and Miller to fire in a shot that Blacklaw did well to turn over the bar. Soon afterwards Bobby went close with an effort.

With Danny staying back, I was able to attack far more than against Leicester City and enjoyed the freedom to roam. Burnley though was a dangerous side with the likes of Jimmy McIlroy, Jimmy Robson and Miller but there was no further score at half time. Bill Nick told us to be alert but carry on playing the same way and more goals would come.

Five minutes after the break their pressure paid off as Burnley equalised when Gordon Harris found Robson with a left wing cross. Robson's low shot went through Bill Brown's legs. It was a blow, but we didn't panic. In fact, the goal pushed us on and we caught Burnley cold within a minute when John White made ground on the left wing before finding Bobby near the penalty spot. A quick turn from Bobby past Miller and a clinical shot past Blacklaw put us back in front. It was a similar goal to the one of he had scored in the Leicester final, bringing the ball down, holding the player off, taking the ball on and volleying it into the back of the net. Bobby's strength got him his Cup final goals.

We urged each other on to get a third, but knew Burnley would not give in. Robson had an effort ruled out for offside before John Connelly went close with a snapshot. Ten minutes from time, Blacklaw dropped a cross and Cummins was forced to handle on the line. Danny made it 3-1 with a lovely penalty, right in the corner giving the keeper no chance.

In recent years, there was the Arsenal fiasco when Pires and Henry made a mess of passing between each other from a spot-kick. Danny and I were going to do the same in the Cup final because we'd practiced it on the training ground. It was all Danny's idea, but that was Danny, always thinking about something a bit different. He was going to knock it to the side and I was to rush in and stick it in the back of the net. Bill Nick didn't know about it as he would not have allowed it, but if the score had been 3-0 or something like that we'd have done it. With the score being 2-1, though, I stayed back on the half-way line because if we'd tried it and I'd missed and we'd lost the FA Cup I'd have been shot! As it turned out Danny stuck it away no problem.

The game was now over and at the final whistle; there were great scenes of celebration. I was particularly pleased for Terry Medwin, who'd missed out against Leicester and obviously Jimmy Greaves in his first final. Second time around you do tend to take more in, but the occasion does go by so quickly. Before we knew it, Danny had lifted the Cup again, the lap of honour was over and the celebrations were beginning. It was a fantastic feeling.

Again, we fancied our chances of performing well in the new season and eventually finished runners-up to Everton in the League, but again entertained, thumping West Ham 6-1, Nottingham Forest 9-2, Manchester United 6-2 and Liverpool 7-2. Burnley avenged the Cup final defeat by knocking us out in the third round of the 1962/63 tournament, while in Europe we became the first British club to win a trophy when we hammered Atletico Madrid 5-1 in the Cup Winner's Cup final in Rotterdam. I played in every round, but missed the final after picking up a pelvic injury playing for Scotland against Austria. I received a medal, but felt sickened to miss out on the final.

A twice broken leg cost me much of the next two seasons as the double team began to break-up. The first fracture came in a European Cup Winner's Cup clash at Old Trafford, the second on my comeback against Shrewsbury Town reserves.

I succeeded Danny as skipper in 1965. It was a hard job because of what Danny had achieved, but also easy because of my personality. I was one of those players that, when I crossed the line, was a captain anyway. It was my nature. Even at 10, I'd be giving orders. If anyone ducked out of a tackle I'd be onto them, "Hey, get your foot in." Everyone hates losing, but I really hate losing. I got so up tight, if anyone let a goal in for nothing I'd go crazy with them. Being skipper suited me.

By 1965/66, the likes of Pat Jennings, Cyril Knowles, Alan Mullery, Jimmy Robertson and Alan Gilzean were making their names. Jimmy Greaves was still slotting in goals for fun and formed a superb partnership with Alan. Any crosses, Alan would nod them down and Jimmy would be onto them in a flash. They were lethal.

In July 1968, Brian Clough persuaded me to sign for Derby County. As with my move to Tottenham, it was just the right time and in my first season, as captain, Derby won the Second Division championship. I also picked up the Footballer of the Year award jointly with Manchester City's captain Tony Book, which was a memorable moment. Following two seasons of top-flight football, I ended my career at Swindon Town.

Looking back, winning the double was a great achievement, but I've always felt that Tottenham should have won the League more than just the once during my time at the club. Our style of play was always to entertain whatever the score and it cost us some games, but we were competitive. On our day, we could and did beat every top team, often scoring bags of goals.

People have often asked me how I'd have adapted to the modern game and the answer is simple, brilliant. It would not have been a problem at all. Whether the current players would have got into our Tottenham side is another matter!

My years at White Hart Lane were special as I was fortunate to play with brilliant players and the camaraderie was excellent. I have so many fond memories, but high up on the list are the three occasions that Tottenham lifted the FA Cup. All three were very special days and ones I will never forget.

PAT JENNINGS
GOALKEEPER 1964–1977

BORN   12 June 1945, Newry, Northern Ireland
SIGNED May 1964 from Watford; £27,000
SPURS CAREER   676 games, 1goal
HONOURS   FA Cup Winner 1967, 1979, League Cup winner 1971, 1973, UEFA Cup 1972, 119 Northern Ireland caps
LEFT Transferred to Arsenal, August 1977; £45,000
RETURNED AS MANAGER 5 March 1984 to 24th May 1985

One of the world's great goalkeepers, Pat Jennings played over 1000 games in a glittering 22-year career. Jennings started out at hometown club Newry Town. A £6,000 fee took him to Watford in May 1963 before joining Spurs, where he claimed FA Cup, League Cup and UEFA Cup winner's medals; he also famously scored in a 1967 Charity Shield thriller against Manchester United and was a UEFA Cup finalist in 1974, before joining North London rivals Arsenal. Footballer of the Year in 1973, Jennings was PFA Player of the Year in 1976, the same year he received an MBE for services to football. Northern Ireland's most celebrated international with 119 caps, he was outstanding in the 1982 and 1986 World Cup finals. A goalkeeping coach at Tottenham since 1993, and briefly, for Northern Ireland, Jennings was inducted to the English Football Hall of Fame in 2003.

Tottenham Hotspur 2 v Chelsea 1

FA Cup Final
Saturday 20 May 1967

Wembley Stadium
Attendance 100,000

Spurs triumph in the first all-London FA Cup final

Teams

Bill Nicholson	**Managers**	Tommy Docherty
Pat Jennings	1	Peter Bonetti
Joe Kinnear	2	Alan Harris
Cyril Knowles	3	Eddie McCreadie
Alan Mullery	4	John Hollins
Mike England	5	Marvin Hinton
Dave Mackay	6	Ron Harris
Jimmy Robertson	7	Charlie Cooke
Jimmy Greaves	8	Tommy Baldwin
Alan Gilzean	9	Tony Hateley
Terry Venables	10	Bobby Tambling
Frank Saul	11	John Boyle
Robertson 45, Saul 67	**Scorers**	Tambling 86

Referee: K Dagnal

I ENJOYED MANY HIGHLIGHTS during my professional football career in both the domestic and international arenas, and among the great stadiums I played at was Wembley. As a one-off, appearing in a cup final or for Northern Ireland in an international was always special. In six finals at the Twin Towers for Tottenham Hotspur and Arsenal, I came away a winner on four occasions, which was fantastic.

Growing up in Newry, I didn't dream about becoming a professional footballer because Gaelic football was the main sport. At Abbeycrombie Junior School, then St Joseph Intermediate School, I played midfield, which would in the future benefit me as I was jumping, challenging players and catching the ball continually. Like lots of kids, I enjoyed football and after school, we would throw down a couple of coats for goals. I went in goal, probably, because I enjoyed throwing myself about and if we didn't have enough players for an 11-a-side or five-a-side match, a few mates would try and score goals past me. I quickly developed my skills.

I played in a U-19 League when I was 11, but it only ran for one season before reverting to Gaelic football. They were street teams and around 1,000 people watched the matches. The next day at school, I knew that all my mates had seen me playing with the big boys. I returned to playing Gaelic football for my school until I left at 15 when I began work at a timber mine.

My brother played football for Newry Town. We'd played together in the U-19 League, so he suggested I trained with the team because I might get a game. After a month, I was selected to play. We won the Irish Junior Cup. I moved onto Newry United, who were playing in the Irish B League in Northern Ireland. It went well and the chairman told me he had forwarded my name to try out for the Irish Youth team that was competing in a European tournament in England. A trial match between players from the North and South of Ireland was taking place in Dublin. The best would represent Ireland.

I was 17, and my first reaction was that I'd never been away from home. In fact, I'd never been further south than Dublin or north than Derry.

I played in the trials and must have impressed because I was soon on my way to England where we were based at a Butlin's holiday camp in Bognor Regis. It was incredible; I'd been playing only a few weeks, everything happened so quickly. We played well and met England in the final at Wembley.

I'd heard about Wembley and seen it on television because we watched the FA Cup final every year. We didn't own a set ourselves, so crowded around my aunt's. Cup final day was a highlight of the year. All the kids supported British teams, but we also followed the fortunes of Northern Ireland international Peter McParland because he lived down the road in Chapel Street. Peter starred for Aston Villa and scored two goals when they won the FA Cup in the 1957 final against Manchester United. There was nothing like a big match. When Northern Ireland played at home, my dad somehow got tickets. I loved the atmosphere.

Arriving at Wembley was unbelievable and although we lost the final, it was a tremendous experience. The tournament was a shop window for many players. Of the Irish team, Dave Clements played for Everton, while Sammy Todd went to Burnley. England had John Hollins and Ron Harris on Chelsea's books, Tommy Smith at Liverpool, John Sissons at West Ham and Jon Sammels at Arsenal. Only one English player wasn't signed up.

Playing at Wembley gave me an opportunity because when I got home, Watford and Coventry City from Division 3 approached Newry Town. Jimmy Hill was Coventry manager and Professional Footballers Association chairman, but a deal was done with Watford.

There were four games left in the 1962/63 season. Watford was in trouble, but managed to finish two points clear of the relegated teams. I played the final two games and the next season when we developed into promotion candidates. It was a tremendous battle, but we finished just two points behind Coventry and Crystal Palace. It was bitterly disappointing, but more for established players. I was starting my career and felt an opportunity would arrive.

I didn't have to wait long because our manager, Bill McGarry, who was just starting out in management and went on to be successful at Wolves, told me that Tottenham Hotspur manager Bill Nicholson had enquired about me. I was delighted because Spurs were a top side. Tottenham had won the double in 1960/61, the FA Cup the following year and then the European Cup Winners Cup in 1963, so for me this was the team. I joined in a £27,000 deal.

Bill Nick gave me my debut in the opening game of the 1964/65 season. We defeated Sheffield United 2-0 and I kept my place until the New Year when Bill Brown in the main played. I was pleased how things had gone and particularly enjoyed a 3-1 win against Arsenal in my first derby match against our North London rivals.

I arrived at an exciting time because Tottenham was developing a new team. Cyril Knowles arrived just before me and a number of younger players such as Alan Mullery, Jimmy Robertson, Phil Beal, Alan Gilzean and Frank Saul were making their mark. Jimmy Greaves had arrived a few years earlier and was a fantastic striker. Club captain Dave Mackay missed that season with a broken leg, but was inspirational behind the scenes. Crowds were massive and football was booming. I went with the flow because a couple of years earlier I was playing in the Irish B League. It was a great set up at Tottenham and there was tremendous banter.

Bill Nick and Eddie Baily were the management team and made sure we were a well-disciplined club. Bill Nick was so professional, the training sessions were always enjoyable and he put together training programmes that still occur 40 years on. Bill Nick was way ahead of his counterparts. I have not heard much new from any manager since, but one major improvement is that there are now specialist goalkeeping coaches.

At Tottenham, I had no goalkeeping coach. When I joined Arsenal in 1977, Bob Wilson came in twice a week. This was the first time I had specialist coaching and I was in my early 30s. Arsenal was one of the first clubs to go down this route. Today, all clubs have followed suit. At Tottenham, now Hans Segers is full time; I assist and love the involvement. Training has improved handling, catching, angles, kicking, in fact everything a goalkeeper does in a match.

In the early part of my career, goalkeepers were only used for practice matches or shooting practice, but it was never what we wanted, it was what forwards wanted. All players did the same training. Nowadays when out-field players go off to develop skills goalkeepers do specialist exercises. It may sound amazing, but the three goalkeepers in Tottenham's squad went to a corner of the field, knocked the ball to one another and just worked on a few things.

Back in the summer of 1965, though, it was an exciting time for me because not only was I playing professional football at the highest level for one of the best sides in the country, but I was earning great money in comparison to what I was earning when cutting timber in the mines. I went from £5 a week to £25 at Watford and £40 at Tottenham, which was far higher than the average working wage. It was fantastic, but we knew how lucky we were because not so long before, footballers were earning a maximum weekly wage of £20.

By now, I had gained my first full cap for Northern Ireland, which was a great honour. I made my debut alongside George Best against Wales in 1964. We had the likes of George and Derek Dougan, but there was little strength in depth so we struggled against big nations. I was busy, which pushed my skills to the limit, but maybe I was too busy at times.

During the 1965/66 campaign, again I shared the goalkeeping duties with Bill Brown. Bill began the season in goal before I played in a televised match on *Match of the Day*, which was in its second season and proving popular with supporters. We thumped defending champions Manchester United who had the likes of Bobby Charlton, Denis Law and George Best in their side 5-1. It was a brilliant performance and we got rave reviews. I also played a few weeks later when they hammered us 5-1 at Old Trafford, a match also televised.

These games, a 4-3 win over Fulham and 5-5 draw with Aston Villa in consecutive home matches summed up attacking football in the mid-60s, but it also illustrated Tottenham's inconsistency. However, we always played football if possible. That was our style, Tottenham supporters expected it but we were shipping goals and had to tighten up.

The draw at home to Villa was particularly frustrating because we were 5-1 up at half time and would have lost in the last minute if Alan Mullery had not stopped a shot on the line. I also played in the FA Cup for the first time and after wins over Middlesbrough and Burnley, Preston knocked us out, which was particularly disappointing as they were in Division 2. It was an upset and illustrated how unpredictable the competition could be.

Following the World Cup, we returned for pre-season training. England's success created tremendous excitement for the new campaign. Every pre-season I never had a problem. I was always in the top six in sprinting and exercises. I was about to cement my place in the first team, while Mike England and Joe Kinnear would become regulars in defence alongside skipper Dave Mackay, now fully fit again and Terry Venables in midfield. Because of the double team, expectations among supporters were always high. There was pressure on the players and Bill Nick to win a trophy or finish in the top three. Although no honours had come our way since the 1963 Cup Winners Cup win, we felt confident and Bill Nick expected us to be challenging.

We began well in 1966/67 and enjoyed our best opening to a League campaign since my arrival. Among eight victories in the opening 11 League fixtures we defeated Leeds United 3-1 on the opening day, Manchester United and Manchester City 2-1, and Fulham 4-3. Jimmy Greaves, despite his bitter disappointment in missing the World Cup final due to injury, was on fire scoring in seven successive games. Our first home defeat came against Blackpool, a match I missed through injury, and it proved the start of a worrying spell when we lost five games in six matches, but we soon bounced back and sent Tottenham supporters into the New Year on a high following a 4-0 victory over Newcastle United.

We played 4-4-2 with wingers. After the 1966 World Cup we were the first team to use Cyril and Joe as attacking full backs. Bill Nick encouraged us to play one and two-touch football. He preached this week in and week out in training. Joe would be playing like a right-winger, Cyril as a left-winger, but that was Bill Nick, if there was space on the wing, he expected us to exploit it. We had to find and play in space. We also had to be entertaining; it was not good enough to just win.

This season was the first time Spurs played in the League Cup. We lost at West Ham, which was disappointing because, although the competition did not have the history of the FA Cup, it was a way into Europe. For players, it was great facing foreign teams. It was different tactically and a challenge. The final was also at Wembley for the first time, so now our only route was in the FA Cup. To play in a Wembley final was a massive target for all footballers because outside an international match it was the only opportunity.

During January 1967, I married Eleanor Toner, like me from Newry, and following a 2-0 win over Arsenal we lost at title-favourites Manchester United. It was a blow, but we were riding high in the League and looked forward to the FA Cup where we were among the favourites. Playing in a cup match, the atmosphere always had an edge and travelling to lower and non-league clubs in particular was not easy. In the FA Cup, it was tough in early rounds because often pitches were rock hard. It was like playing on the road, the bounce was uneven.

The dangerous thing about a hard or dry pitch was coming out for a cross, especially if you had to get off the ground. People could easily take your legs away and coming down onto a hard or frozen pitch was pretty hazardous. I preferred to punch a ball rather than catch it and try hanging on. Pitches were also watered to make the ball skip along the ground, so

I wore 'Bonetti' or 'Banks' gloves. They were more or less, cotton; there were no 'Super' gloves with plastic grips, which only came in towards the end of my career.

As usual, we had gathered around a radio after training to hear the third round draw and hoped for a home tie. We were reasonably happy with a third round tie at Division Two Millwall. It would be tough, though, and Millwall supporters were sure to be vocal. Playing away to a lower division club was always difficult. There was a capacity crowd rooting for the home team and players drew inspiration from thatt.

It was their cup final. Opposing teams had a real go at home whereas if the match was away, they were more defensive, which suited our style.We warmed up for the match with a 2-0 league win over Burnley and went to the Den in confident mood. We drew 0-0, which was a satisfactory result. Every team needs a bit of luck in a cup competition and we were fortunate. In fact, if Cyril Knowles had not cleared an effort off the line we would have been knocked out. We scraped through the replay a few days later with an Alan Gilzean goal after a mistake by Tom Wilson.

Before the replay, we knew our fourth round opponents and did not complain having to face Division Two outfit Portsmouth at home. A draw at title-chasing Nottingham Forest and win over Fulham kept our spirits up and we came through comfortably against Portsmouth 3-1. Alan Gilzean scored two goals while Jimmy Greaves notched his first goal of the cup run.

The fifth round gave us a home tie against our third consecutive Division Two opponents. The clash with Bristol City came in the middle of a spell of three draws in the League. Jimmy Greaves saw us into the quarter-finals with two goals, one a penalty in a 2-0 win. Reaching the quarter-finals, you know that Wembley is only two matches away and the excitement builds up within the club and among supporters. We had played in front of capacity crowds for all three home games and the atmosphere was tremendous.

Incredibly, the sixth round draw gave us another Division Two team, and our luck was certainly holding to miss the likes of Leeds United, Chelsea and Manchester City. Birmingham now stood in our way and, although we knew it would be a tough battle, as we had to travel, we fancied our chances.

Away from the Cup, we were going well in Division One. The weeks leading to the Birmingham clash saw us pick up four consecutive victories including a double over FA Cup holders Everton and defending champions Liverpool. If you are winning, confidence builds for the next game. Our form was no surprise to me as we were developing into a cracking team and we needed to, having to face the likes of Manchester United, Liverpool, Leeds United, Arsenal, Chelsea, Everton and Manchester City every week.

A bumper crowd was guaranteed for the trip to St. Andrew's and as expected, we had to battle hard, but were satisfied with a 0-0 draw. We ran away with the replay 6-0. Jimmy Greaves and Terry Venables scored two goals each, while Alan Gilzean and Frank Saul also found the target. Birmingham had their best chance in the first game, but failed to take it.

We knew that whomever we drew in the semi-finals was going to be a cracking tie. It turned out to be Nottingham Forest, who alongside Leeds United and ourselves were chasing Manchester United at top of the table. Forest had fine players in Frank Wignall, Ian Storey-Moore and Terry Hennessey, but we felt confident of winning as we were in the midst of an unbeaten run. In the other clash, Chelsea faced Leeds. The expectation among Tottenham supporters was enormous because we had not been in a semi-final for five years. Two more League victories came our way as our winning sequence stretched to six before the semi-final at Hillsborough.

The pressure was intense on match day. Nobody wants to lose a semi-final because of all the effort in previous ties. On the day, Forest striker Frank Wignall had to be replaced following a Dave Mackay challenge. Frank was a key player for Forest, so it was a big loss for them. Jimmy Greaves and Frank Saul scored, which proved enough as we reached Wembley with a 2-1 victory. Terry Hennessey scored late on for Forest, but it was too late.

There was both relief and joy at reaching Wembley. This would be the first major final for most of our team, including me of course. Over the years, I experienced winning and losing semi-finals and finals. Losing a semi-final is by far the worst feeling, more so than a final. Losing at Wembley is dreadful, but at least you have the day. For the first time in modern history, there would be an all-London final as Chelsea edged out Leeds United 1-0 in the other semi-final.

Talk among fans was now about the final and we ended the league season superbly with three victories from four games to finish third and qualify for the Fairs Cup [the predecessor of the UEFA Cup]. Jimmy Greaves scored in wins over Sunderland, West Ham and Sheffield United, but not even a run of nine wins from our final 10 games was enough to catch champions Manchester United, who finished four points clear. Nottingham Forest edged us out of second spot on goal average. I was surprised Forest did so well because they just avoided relegation a year before, but credit to them.

We now had a week to prepare for the final against Chelsea, who, in the league, had defeated us 3-0 at Stamford Bridge before drawing 1-1 at White Hart Lane. Managed by Tommy Docherty, Chelsea had terrific players like midfielder John Hollins and fearsome defenders Ron 'Chopper' Harris and Eddie McCreadie and could beat anyone on their day. Nevertheless, we were in great form and fancied our chances. Local media analysed every possible angle and supporters were desperate for tickets. Everywhere we went; fans asked how we thought the game would go. As Peter McParland experienced with Aston Villa in 1957 there was plenty of encouragement from my hometown Newry in letters, which was a great boost.

During the week, training was kept the same as in previous rounds. Our schedule went well at Cheshunt as we kept sharp before staying on the Friday night at a West End Hotel. We went to see 'The Professionals' at a local cinema and Bill Nick gave the main team talk. Chelsea also had a great goalkeeper in Peter Bonetti. Then there was winger Charlie Cooke, who could cause a lot of trouble, while in attack Tony Hateley and Bobby Tambling would have to be tightly marked.

For all Chelsea had to offer, I was confident because we had a great side. Joe Kinnear was very steady, a good tackler and passer of the ball. Joe was one of those lucky lads who never lost a final and used to brag about it! Joe was a cocky Jack-the-Lad. Cyril Knowles had a brilliant left peg and could run all day. Cyril's tackling frightened the life out of the best wingers and he would be the one who'd have to keep Charlie Cooke quiet.

There was no better centre-half around than Mike England. He could tackle, pass, score headed goals and was one of those players that was first on the team sheet. Mike was a born leader and captained his country Wales, as well as later managing them. As for Dave Mackay, he was a fantastic captain. Dave had moved back into defence by the time I arrived at Spurs. He inspired us to perform and drove us on. Dave was a tremendous tackler, a fearsome competitor and simply did not know the meaning of defeat.

Alan Mullery was a great player. We called him the Tank; he was such a strong tackler, and got up and down the field. Terry Venables had good ball control and was a nice passer. Terry liked to get it, look around, then pass it but when we needed to take the heat out of a game, he also played that role brilliantly. Terry was also the Mickey taker, a real Jack-the-Lad and had begun his career at Chelsea, only moving to White Hart Lane the previous summer, so there was a bit of needle there.

Winger Jimmy Robertson was unbelievably quick. When Jimmy got the ball, he had strength and pace to beat defenders and create chances. Jimmy reduced pressure towards the end of a match by keeping the ball away from our goal. On the left wing, during the cup run Frank Saul had replaced Cliff Jones, who played in Tottenham's FA Cup wins in the early 1960s along with Dave Mackay. Frank was an unsung hero. At another club, Frank would have been a real superstar.

As a strike partnership, Alan Gilzean and Jimmy Greaves were among the best around. Dubbed the G-Men, they led the line brilliantly. Alan was a superb target man. For me it was brilliant because I could always pick him out with my clearances up field. Alan was a clever player, strong in the air, on the ground and was a good all round forward.

Jimmy Greaves was the most clinical finisher I played with during my career and I've not seen anyone since better. He had a great finishing technique. When Jimmy was one on one with a goalkeeper, he would not shoot immediately, he would let the keeper commit himself then slide it by him on the other side. Jimmy never hammered them in; he would pass them in to the net. Many times also, he would pick up a knockdown from Alan on the halfway line, set off on a dribble and score a great solo goal. Jimmy had everything, he was superb at scoring overhead kicks and was a great header of the ball; people often forget that. Jimmy was a complete natural and not just a goal scorer, often he'd link up play. People thought of him as brilliant only in the penalty box, but he could score from anywhere. Nobody could touch Jimmy Greaves.

On the morning of the match, I went for a walk with Alan Mullery, thinking through some of the points from our team talk. After a pre-match meal, it was time to depart for Wembley. Going down Wembley Way in the bus, it really was great seeing supporters dressed up in both team colours, but by then I was already focussing on the game. At the ground, we walked around the stadium before changing in the enormous dressing rooms. I was only 21, but luckily I'd played internationals at Wembley, so knew what the atmosphere and noise would be like. For others it was a first experience and it does hit you.

In the dressing room, I looked around and felt confident. Dave Mackay knew what it took to win. Bill Nick also had seen it all before. He came around each player with a reminder of what he expected and words of encouragement. For me it concerned Chelsea's wingers, when they liked to get crosses in and whether they cut inside to get shots in. I also had to watch out for the centre-forward, Tony Hateley, who was strong in the air and the midfield men coming through from midfield.

Thirty minutes before kick-off there was a heavy shower, but conditions were perfect on a sunny day. Walking out on to the pitch, I reflected on seeing players enjoying the moment and thought, how lucky I was, but we had to perform. I could not wait for the game to get started. After being presented to the dignitaries, we warmed up before the roar went up from supporters for the kick-off.

We were most pundits' favourites, but knew it would be a tough match. During the opening period, our plan to utilise Alan Gilzean's aerial strength worked well and we gained the early initiative. Facing Marvin Hinton, Alan's flicks caused Chelsea all sorts of problems. Ron Harris marked Jimmy Greaves tightly, but that brought opportunities and we went close to scoring several times. Alan and Jimmy sent Joe Kinnear clear, but his cross was too deep. Frank Saul then went close with a half volley from a great cross by Alan Mullery before Peter Bonetti had to be at his best to keep out a left-foot shot by Jimmy Robertson. Frank then headed wide when well placed.

Chelsea had a reputation as a physical side, but failed to get at us and, in Wembley's open spaces, Jimmy Robertson and Frank Saul had room to cause damage. The way the teams were set up Chelsea had a man advantage in midfield, but early on Charlie Cooke was unable to get in a telling cross, while Tony Hateley found it impossible to shake off Mike England.

John Hollins was Chelsea's best player and I had to dive at two players' feet when he put in a great cross-shot from 25 yards. Jimmy Greaves then went close, before I was back in action after a great dribble by Charlie Cooke and just managed push to his shot past the post. Jimmy again almost broke the deadlock with a terrific free-kick, bending the ball around the wall only to see it go inches wide. Late in the half, I tipped another Cooke effort over the bar. The score was 0-0, so it wasan important stop because the first goal is crucial in any cup final.

Just before half time, we finally made the breakthrough after John Boyle was penalised. From the free-kick, Alan Mullery swept forward and had a strike at goal from distance. The ball struck Chelsea skipper Ron Harris and fell to Jimmy Robertson, who made no mistake with a low half-volley into the corner past Bonetti. The goal could not have come at a better time and we went into the interval feeling great. For Chelsea, it must have been a bitter blow.

We started the second half in confident mood and Chelsea struggled to break us down. They did go close when Hateley headed just over, but I felt another goal would come for us. Jimmy Greaves was just wide with a snap shot that almost caught Bonetti out before Frank Saul doubled our lead on 67 minutes. Dave Mackay floated a long throw in towards the danger area. Jimmy Robertson flicked the ball across the penalty area to Frank Saul, who swivelled brilliantly before hooking the ball past a surprised Bonetti in one movement. It was a fantastic goal worthy of winning the Cup.

In control, we nearly added a third, but Joe Kinnear's cross failed to reach Frank at the far post. Chelsea tried to hit back, but they knew it was all over. We slowed the game down then and, after Hateley headed over, I misjudged a long cross by Boyle with four minutes remaining. I could have left the ball to our defenders, but didn't. I got a nick on the cross, but Bobby Tambling headed in a soft goal to give Chelsea hope. It was a blow, but we were in no mood to let them back into the game.

I knew that there was not long remaining. It was a matter of keeping concentration and we comfortably played the remaining minutes out without too many problems. At the final whistle, there was sheer joy to have won. For the club it was a third triumph of the 60s. No side was more successful in the competition during the decade. For me it was my first FA Cup winner's medal. It was an unbelievable moment; I was so delighted. We were the better team on the day and played within ourselves. Chelsea caused occasional problems, we weren't at our most fluent and it may not have been a classic final, but we thoroughly deserved the win.

After we all congratulated each other, it was time to go up the famous steps to receive the trophy and collect our winner's medals. Over the years, I'd seen so many players go up on television, now it was my turn. It was a marvellous moment when Dave lifted the Cup. Then we passed the trophy around on the lap of honour as supporters sang their hearts out before we carried on our celebrations in the dressing room.

In the evening, we attended a banquet. Over 100,000 supporters lined the route as we went on an open top bus along Tottenham High Road for a civic reception to Tottenham Town Hall. It was a memorable few days. In the summer, I headed back to Ireland to show everyone at home my winner's medal.

We shared the Charity Shield with League Champions Manchester United following a memorable curtain raiser to the 1967/68 campaign, when I scored my only goal for Tottenham with a massive clearance that bounced over Alex Stepney's head in a 3-3 draw and was confident of further trophy success. I hoped to return to Wembley when our FA Cup defence started and was delighted when we overcame Manchester United in a third round replay, but Liverpool knocked us out in the fifth round. Sadly, we only reached the FA Cup quarter-finals a couple of times over the coming years.

We did win the League Cup at Wembley against Aston Villa in 1971 and Norwich City in 1973. Both were memorable events, but neither was the same as winning the FA Cup. The League Cup was less glamorous; the final was not live on television, but playing at Wembley was always special. We won the UEFA Cup in 1972, which was great, but some glamour was taken away because we played Wolves in the final. It wasn't quite the same playing against an English club as it just felt like a normal league game. We defeated fashionable European teams on the way and reached the final again in 1974, but lost to Feyenoord.

At the end of 1976/77, my contract was up. I had an ankle injury and Barry Daines had done well, but I was hopeful of a new contract. I would carry on because fitness was not a problem. When a contract was not offered, it was a shock. Although Tottenham meant a lot to me, it was time to move on. During the close season, I more or less accepted an offer to join Bobby Robson at Ipswich Town, who were one of the best club sides around at that time. Bobby saw me as the missing part to a good team that included Mick Mills, Brian Talbot, Alan Brazil, Paul Mariner and Clive Woods, but the deal fell through when striker Trevor Wymark broke a leg, as they had to strengthen the attack instead.

While I considered options from a number of clubs, it was made clear to me that I was not wanted at Tottenham – even to train – as it would be an embarrassment to other goalkeepers. So I said "cheerio" to the players and staff. Tottenham directors ignored me, which was some thanks after 14 years' service. At that point, I decided to join Arsenal as it would cause most embarrassment to directors. If any of them had rung to wish me luck, I'd have gone to another club, maybe a London club, but not Arsenal. The directors could not have hurt me more and even insisted on selling me for a profit when other long-serving players like Mike England and Ralph Coates left on free transfers. I felt very let down by the club, but sad for Tottenham supporters, who obviously weren't pleased that I'd moved to Highbury.

On the international scene, representing Northern Ireland, we enjoyed some fantastic results, especially at Wembley when we defeated England in the Home Internationals in 1972 and drew to qualify for the 1986 World Cup finals. I was 36 at my first World Cup in 1982 when we beat host nation Spain to qualify for the second round. I chose to bow out at the highest level against Brazil on my 41st birthday in the 1986 finals. I could have carried on, but decided that there was no further to go.

Looking back at my career, I was very fortunate because I had a fantastic rapport with fans at every club, but particularly at Tottenham. That was probably because, being a goalkeeper, I was so near to them. If you are doing the business then you are the hero, if not then you are in trouble. I remember going to Highbury after winning the Footballer of the Year award in 1973 and receiving a terrific ovation, which was unheard of for a Tottenham player.

Personal awards were special, but for players it was all about winning major honours. I collected five winners' medals and the FA Cup triumphs were particularly special. The win with Tottenham in 1967 still means so much to me, as it was my first. I was so fortunate as many players never had that opportunity. Winning the FA Cup was fantastic and it will always have that touch of glamour. I would not swap my winner's medals for anything.

STEVE PERRYMAN
MIDFIELDER/DEFENDER 1969–1986

BORN 21 December 1951, Ealing
SIGNED January 1969, from apprentice
SPURS CAREER 866 appearances, 39 goals
HONOURS FA Cup Winner 1981, 1982, UEFA Cup Winner 1972, League Cup Winner 1971, 1973, 1 full England cap
LEFT Free transfer to Oxford United, 25 March 1986

Tottenham's record appearance maker and captain for nearly 10 years, Steve Perryman is a true Spurs legend and can consider himself unlucky not to have added to his solitary full England cap. He famously led Spurs to consecutive FA Cup wins in the early 80s from full-back, but his most memorable game came as a 20 year-old midfield destroyer – and, on this occasion, goalscorer.

Tottenham Hotspur 2 v AC Milan 1

UEFA Cup semi-final first leg
Monday 5 April 1972

White Hart Lane
Attendance: 42,064

*Young destroyer turns goalscorer to set up a famous victory and send
Spurs on their way to a first UEFA cup triumph*

Teams

Bill Nicholson	**Managers**	Nereo Rocco
Pat Jennings	1	Fabio Cudicini
Joe Kinnear	2	Giuseppe Sabadini
Cyril Knowles	3	Guilio Zignoli
Ralph Coates	4	Angelo Anquilletti
Mike England	5	Karl-Heinz Schnellinger
Terry Naylor	6	Roberto Rosato
Alan Gilzean	7	Riccardo Sogliano
Steve Perryman	8	Romeo Benetti
Martin Chivers	9	Albertino Bigon
Martin Peters	10	Gianni Rivera
Alan Mullery	11	Lino Golin
Perryman 33, 64	**Scorers**	Benetti 25
	Sent Off	Sogliano 63

Referee: Mariano Medina Iglesias (Spain)

MOST MEMORABLE GAME for Spurs? I don't have to think too much about that. It has to be the first leg of the 1972 UEFA Cup semi-final, when we beat AC Milan 2-1 at White Hart Lane. I've even got a tape of the game at home. I can lend it to you if you like, just don't lose it whatever you do, because it's very precious to me. It's the only way I can get some people to believe me when I tell them I scored twice in one game! Obviously you don't win games just by scoring goals – it's a team effort. But on this occasion I got the headlines, which didn't happen very often given my position and role in the team, so it really sticks in the memory.

I'd scored goals for Tottenham before, of course, but only nine prior to that game, and I only managed 39 in total during my White Hart Lane career. That was the first time in my professional career that I scored twice in a match and it only happened twice more. Christ, as time went on I didn't even score twice a season most of the time! So to score two very good goals in such a big game, against such a good side to win the tie and reach a Cup final, was very special for me. For some reason, it was my night.

What makes it extra special is that we went on to beat Wolves in the first all-English European final. It was Spurs' second European trophy and the first ever UEFA Cup, as its name had been changed from the Inter Cities Fairs Cup. Although I was club captain eight years later when we won the UEFA Cup for a second time, I was suspended for the second leg of the final against Anderlecht, so 1972 was the only time I was in the team when we lifted the trophy.

I'd won two League Cups and a UEFA Cup by the time I was 21, but I actually came to fruition as a footballer fairly late. I played for my district until I was 11, but then I went to a grammar school where they didn't play competitive football. The sports master was a basketball coach, so we played that instead. Then he went on a 'refresher' course for a year and the chap who replaced him saw me play football and said he was going to put me forward for the district team once again. I got in, and by the start of the 1966/67 season I was in the England Schools team.

All of the other lads in the England team had been signed by clubs when they were 11 or 12, so I was the player all the scouts were after. Bill Nicholson, Ron Greenwood, Malcolm Allison – you name them, I had them all round my house chasing my signature. When it came to the crunch, I wanted to go to QPR because they were my team. My brother said I should go to West Ham. England had just won the World Cup and he said Hurst, Moore and Peters would teach me how to play football. But my dad wanted me to go to Tottenham – and he would eventually get his way.

Spurs were the first club to knock on my door and I used to train with them regularly before I actually signed, and although my dad wasn't a Spurs fan, they always treated him well when I went for trials. Unlike some of the other clubs I trained with, Tottenham never tried to force me to sign anything. They would let me go off and train with other clubs if I wanted to and I liked that. By this point my work was suffering with all the football I was playing and the school were going ape-shit, but my mind was made up that I wanted to be a footballer.

It was coming to the end of the 1966/67 season and Spurs were playing Chelsea in the FA Cup final. I got a call from Tommy Docherty, the Chelsea manager, inviting me to the game. He arranged for a chauffeur-driven car to pick up me and my family, take us to Wembley and meet the players in the dressing room afterwards – "when we've won the Cup," he said. There was no mention of signing for Chelsea.

A few days later I was at a training session with Spurs and Bill Nick just happened to be there. He saw me, walked up to me and said, "Steve, are you going to fucking sign for us, or what?" It was a big decision for a kid to make. Scouts would do so much to persuade you to sign for them rather than somebody else. My mum used to have packets of biscuits sent to her, I was invited to play golf. Jesus, one scout even came round and offered to cut our lawn! But nobody could persuade me like Bill Nick. That was typical of him. He was straightforward. No kidology, no mind games, no bollocks – and that was an approach that I responded to.

He told me that they'd coach me right, treat me fair and that, if I was good enough, I'd get my chance, and if I wasn't they would help me find another club. I could have taken money to go somewhere else, but my dad told me that money wasn't important at that stage and he was right. In the end Spurs got me for nothing.

Bill was never quick to part with the club's money. Early in my career I was sharing a room with Alan Gilzean and we were discussing wages. It turned out he was earning a lot more than me – £95 a week to my £18 a week – and he told me I should go and ask Bill for a raise, knowing exactly what would happen. Eventually I plucked up enough courage to go and ask him. He didn't look up at me once. "How much do you want?" he said. "Twenty pounds a week," I said. "Twenty pounds a week?!" he replied. "Have you ever seen yourself fucking play?" I did get my raise in the end, but I think that was just his way of putting me in my place.

I signed professional terms in January 1969, just after my 17th birthday, and by the start of the 1969/70 season I was in the first team squad. To be honest I didn't expect things to happen so quickly, but I had a bit of luck, which you sometimes need in football.

I'd only played six games for the reserve team when I was taken on a pre-season tour to North America with the first team. As a youth team player, you didn't really get to know the first team and you knew your place. The original plan was for me to go on tour, be involved in the first game, at which point Alan Gilzean would join up with the squad after being on international duty with Scotland and I would fly home.

After the first game against Aston Villa in Baltimore we were all told to go out, enjoy ourselves and have the following day off. But David Jenkins, another young lad who had played a few first team games the previous season and was ahead of me in the pecking order, got sunburn on the top of his feet. He couldn't train the next day because he couldn't do his boots up! Well, you can imagine how well that went down with Bill Nicholson – he went ape-shit!

So, rather than being sent home when Gilly arrived, I stayed out there with the rest of the squad. We played West Ham in Atlanta – they had Hurst, Moore and Peters playing for them and this really was a whole new experience for me – then we went on to Toronto, where we played Everton and Glasgow Rangers in a mini-tournament. I ended up playing every game and it looked like I'd put myself in contention for place in the first team for the new season.

The last Tuesday before the start of the season was a press day. The first team would play the reserve team on one pitch and the 'A' team would play the youth team on the other. If you didn't get into any of those teams, you knew you were in trouble. Lining up in the first team when there were 22 and 23-year-olds who couldn't even get in the reserves, standing there watching from the sidelines was pretty intimidating. Although I didn't make my debut until 27th September, I ended up playing 27 games that season and stayed in the team for nearly 17 years!

Bill Nick usually signed one big player every year. From 1964 onwards, Spurs signed Alan Mullery, Pat Jennings, Terry Venables, Mike England and Martin Chivers in consecutive years and, being a big, successful club with good finances, the big players who were already there rarely left unless they were past their best.

But Bill didn't make any big signings at the start of the 1969/70 season. I don't think that had anything to do with me, but by the time Martin Peters joined from West Ham towards the end of the season – with Jimmy Greaves going the other way – I'd managed to establish myself in the team.

I think what got me noticed in the first place was my natural talent and the fact that I played with a lot of freedom. At the time I was really more of an inside-forward than a midfielder. I could pass, I could move, I had good vision and an eye for goal. I never had great pace and could never really beat men, but I could certainly pass it around them.

But when I initially got into the Spurs first team, they were struggling, especially in midfield. Dave Mackay had left for Derby County a year earlier, Terry Venables had moved on and they had even tried playing Greavesie in midfield, which seems unbelievable in retrospect. Basically, at that stage, Alan Mullery was the midfield, almost on his own.

Having lost 5-0 at Derby the previous week, they drafted me and Dennis Bond in for the next game against Sunderland. Dennis had been bought from Watford a couple of seasons earlier and was a few years older than me. He was a fantastic footballer, but perhaps not quite mobile enough to be a top, top player. Me, on the other hand – I just couldn't stop running. And because I was young and impressionable, if someone said, "run from there to there," I would. The team already had too many chiefs and not enough Indians, so I was thrown in there as a designated Indian!

One day I closed down an opposition midfield player. He passed the ball to their right wing and I instinctively followed it, even though I knew it was somebody else's responsibility. I was just so full of running. Their winger passed the ball back to the central midfielder, so back I went. Again, the central midfielder knocked it out to the wing, and by this point I was looking out for our left-back Cyril Knowles, but all I can hear is him shouting, "go on, cock", which is the Northern equivalent of "go on, mate." I was thinking "fucking hell," but I chased the ball down again. "Go on cock," Knowlesy kept shouting. I stopped, turned around and said, "You mean 'go on, prick', don't ya?"

That non-stop approach didn't do me any good in the long-term, because I got a reputation as a runner and a tackler and that wasn't really what my game was about. But once you've started giving those things to a team, you can't take them away.

You've got to remember, the game was changing at this time. Up until 1966, most teams were playing 4-2-4, which was a great system if it worked, but if you were having a bad day you could get murdered. For example, in the 1967/68 season, my first as an apprentice, Spurs lost 5-1 at Burnley, then beat them 5-0 at White Hart Lane a few months later with almost exactly the same team.

Alf Ramsey's 4-4-2 'Wingless Wonders' were the blueprint now. Players like Alan Ball and Nobby Stiles were the new breed of midfield player and I was moulded into one of them during my first season in the team. I very much had to learn on the job. Not only could I not retract those qualities, but they couldn't leave me out either, because I worked harder than anybody else.

For two years, I swear I couldn't do a thing wrong. Even if I just cleared the ball and Jimmy Greaves or Martin Chivers picked it up on the halfway line, beat three men and scored, according to the press, I'd made the goal! It was like I had the Midas touch. Yet I never really rated myself that highly. I had this horrible, hunched running style and hated watching myself on television, but when things were going well, people were saying I'd play for England before I was 22, and so on.

Then, in my third season, I went up for a header in a game against Liverpool and came down hard on my ankle. I carried on playing for weeks, but it didn't feel right. I couldn't move right, I couldn't pressure the ball right, I couldn't even kick it right. Adrenaline got me through games and I got by, but it wasn't right and I was giving the ball away quite a bit. I was in turmoil really. From having everything come so easy to me before, I was suddenly starting to feel the pressure of the crowd and the disappointment when I did something wrong.

Eventually, the ankle got better, but it took longer to heal than it probably should have, because I was playing on it. In those days training was always very hard, so it wasn't like I was getting any kind of rest. As a manager, I would never take a risk with a player. Let them work in the gym or whatever, but never make them do anything that could aggravate the injury. But in those days you just didn't do that – you had to train.

Even though the injury had cleared up, my confidence was still quite low as we headed into the latter part of the 1971/72 season. I hadn't been playing particularly well in the run up to the Milan game, but it turned out to be the match that really put me back on the road to being my old self.

We had a great side by 1971/72. Pat Jennings in goal, Mike England and Cyril Knowles at the back, Gilly and Martin Chivers up front and me, Martin Peters and Alan Mullery in midfield. Even a young Graeme Souness couldn't get the side – and he let Bill know he wasn't happy.

Having struggled a bit in my first season, we finished third in the league in 1971, which meant the club qualified for Europe for the first time in four seasons. We also reached the quarter-final of the FA Cup and won the League Cup, beating Aston Villa 2-0 in the final. So, by the start of the following season, having signed another flair player, Ralph Coates from Burnley, expectations were pretty high. If we couldn't challenge for the title, there was definitely a feeling that we could at least win a cup.

As it turned out, we could have won all three, but we were probably victims of our own success in the end. By December, we were in the semi-finals of the League Cup and the quarter-finals of the UEFA Cup, but the European games in particular really began to take their toll on our league form. You would get back on a Thursday to Luton Airport from wherever you'd been on the Wednesday. In those days, the players would then go out for a drink, which didn't really give your body much time to recover in readiness for the next game on the Saturday. Adrenaline and determination to win got us through a lot of the time, but it wasn't always enough.

We didn't win a league game over Christmas and New Year. That pretty much put us out of contention and we ended up finishing sixth, only seven points behind champions Derby County in what was a closely-contested title race that year. Chelsea knocked us out of the League Cup in the first weekend in January and after we lost to eventual winners Leeds in the quarter-final of the FA Cup in March, we were able to concentrate on the UEFA Cup.

After beating Icelandic side Keflavik 15-1 on aggregate in the first round, we had a tough draw against Nantes in the second round. We managed to scrape a 0-0 draw out there, but we were lucky to get away with it, and we weren't much better at White Hart Lane, where Martin Peters scored the only goal of the game. Nantes played in a completely different way to any other team we'd faced and we just weren't at the races that day.

It was during that season, of course, that Hunter Davies followed the team around for his classic book *The Glory Game*. I don't remember much of Hunter being around, mainly because I was just a young lad who pretty much kept himself to himself, and he tended to concentrate on the main 'social flow' of the team. Obviously he mentions me in the book, and he came round my mum's house, where I still lived, to interview me for the appendix, but I didn't have a whole chapter dedicated to me like a lot of the other players.

Anyway, it emerged later that after the Nantes game was the one time Bill really wished Hunter Davies hadn't been in the room, because he really wanted to let rip at the players. I remember, just before the book was released, Bill calling a meeting and turning up with a load of rough copies. "You stupid bastards," he said. "Take a pencil and cross out what you don't want in there."

As pleased as I am because *The Glory Game* is part of our history, I could never work out how they let it happen. At the time, Spurs were one of the hardest clubs to get access to. Bill didn't seek publicity, neither did the club. They were one of the last to put advertising in their programme or around the ground and were almost backward about promoting themselves. They felt they didn't need to. Even celebrity fans like Warren Mitchell and Peter Cook didn't get complimentary tickets.

Dinamo Bucharest were expected to provide another difficult hurdle in the next round, but we won easily 5-0 on aggregate. Although that looks straightforward enough on paper, it doesn't quite tell the whole story. After winning 3-0 at home, our trip to Bucharest was anything but comfortable. The hotel was OK, but the stadium was a vast concrete bowl only about a quarter full, the dressing rooms were some of the worst I've seen and Bucharest just seemed intent on kicking us off the park, especially once they realised they had no real chance of getting back in the tie. Bill told us what to expect, but nothing ever prepares you for that. Martin Chivers and Gilly came in for the worst treatment, being kicked, punched and elbowed off the ball, but I suffered the most, falling badly on my shoulder and dislocating it. It popped straight back in and I insisted on carrying on, but I had to come off at half-time. We eventually won 2-0.

There was a three-month break before the quarter-finals, where we played another Romanian team, UT Arad. We won 2-0 over there, then came the FA Cup loss to Leeds. I think that knocked the stuffing out of us a bit, as we were fairly off colour in the return leg against Arad, but the tie was effectively won by then and a 1-1 draw at home put us through to the semi-final against AC Milan. It was seen as a real glamour tie.

European competitions didn't involve as many clubs in those days so there weren't many massive games, but Milan were a genuinely great side, one of the best in Europe. Five of the players had been in the team that won the European Cup in 1969, including Gianni Rivera, the playmaker, who had also played in the 1970 World Cup Final, along with Rosato. It was my job to look after Rivera. Then there was Romeo Benetti, who they called 'The Englishman', because he was so big and strong, and at the back you had Karl-Heinz Schnellinger, the German, who played against England in the 1966 World Cup Final.

But whereas these days teams know each other like the back of their hands because of TV and extended competition formats, our knowledge of European opposition was limited. We had a dossier on Milan, with pictures of their players and how they played, but there were no videos. As for watching them play, Bill would have done that occasionally, but flying to places like Milan was much more difficult then than it is today. Today, you can fly from any number of airports at various times quite cheaply, but in them days you could probably only fly from Heathrow and the flights weren't that often and were more expensive. Unlike in today's Champions League, you wouldn't play teams that often, either.

What we did know was that the Italians were great defenders and if you went behind against them, you were up against it. That said, we didn't prepare any differently. We knew their approach wouldn't be the same as an English side, but we didn't go in with any specific plans.

The first leg at White Hart Lane was our eighth game in the space on 18 days, so we knew exactly how we were going to play and it was just a case of keeping ourselves ticking over. It sounds like a lot, but I remember thinking, "I'd rather be playing than training", because with Bill Nick and Eddie Baily, Christ did we train! If you did an hour and a half's training, it would be an hour and a half's proper work: running, weights, sit-ups – and that's not even counting the warm up and warm down. But you can't train that hard and play that many games and they were intelligent enough to know that. I'm just glad that I was young, naïve and full of desire and I think the fact that I was playing in a successful team saw me through.

Our hectic schedule did take it's toll in terms of injuries, though, and the day before the away leg Alan Mullery was recalled from a loan spell at Fulham after John Pratt had broken his nose, and Mullers went straight back into the team as captain.

He'd been a very successful player for Spurs, but he'd picked up a pelvic injury earlier in the season and by the time it had cleared up, we had a settled side. Bill never liked to change a winning team, so Mullers was sent out on loan to stay fit. I don't think he was happy about it, and I think there was a bit of a falling out. I don't know what happened exactly, but things certainly weren't right between them. Due to the injury crisis, though, they had no choice but to call him back. It proved to be a bit of a masterstroke.

A European night at White Hart Lane was something else. There'd be 50,000 packed in and they would be yours for the night. Spurs fans get called fickle, but in away games we would set out to keep the ball for the first 20 minutes and if the opposition hadn't created a chance, the crowd would get on their backs. We didn't have that problem – our fans always gave you absolutely everything.

That first leg was certainly a different type of game. It didn't have the ebb and flow of an English game. Even though we had the wind in our faces, we just attacked and attacked in the first half. We always looked dangerous, especially from crosses. Martin Chivers headed over in the first few minutes and Martin Peters also had a decent chance after I put in a cross from deep.

When Milan did win the ball, they tried to catch us on the break and it was from one of those quick attacks that they opened the scoring – and what a goal it was. Rivera fed the hard man, Benetti, and before Pat Jennings even had a chance to set himself, the ball flew into the top corner from 25 yards. It was a great goal.

I remember thinking, "we're up against it here", because the Italians were masters at closing out a game and they would have been delighted with a 1-0 lead going into the second leg. Now Milan just sat back even more, whereas we really had to give it a go and win the game. But like I said, the crowd stayed with us, which was a big boost, and we were back level within seven minutes.

One of the criticisms of me had always been that I didn't shoot enough, and that when I did, I didn't hit the target often enough. But that wasn't really my job. I was essentially a defensive midfield player and my job was to cover for other players when they went forward, so I was rarely in a position to shoot, but because we were desperate to force an equaliser, I pushed up a bit more.

As the ball came across from the right, Martin Peters was about to take it on the run and go into the penalty area. I was stood right behind him and shouted for him to leave it, which he did. There were loads of players around me, so I didn't really have time to think. I hit it first time from the edge of the box and caught it sweetly. It was still rising as it got to the goal and, although Fabio Cudicini [Chelsea goalkeeper Carlo's dad] managed to get his fingertips on it, it was right in corner and he could only help it on its way. It was a good strike and the crowd went mad.

I hit the deck (white no.9) as I beat Gordon Banks in the Leicester
goal to put us one up. It was my dream to score in the FA Cup final.
To win the double at the same time was incredible.

Parading the Cup around
Wembley with skipper Danny
Blanchflower (left).

Celebrating victory with my
wife at the after-match party at
the Savoy Hotel.

Celebrating the first goal of my hat-trick which put us 3-1 ahead
on the night and drew us level 4-4 on aggregate with Gornik.

Our fifth goal flies in past keeper Kostka from the head of Bobby Smith.
This goal put us 7-5 ahead on aggregate and broke Gornik's hearts.

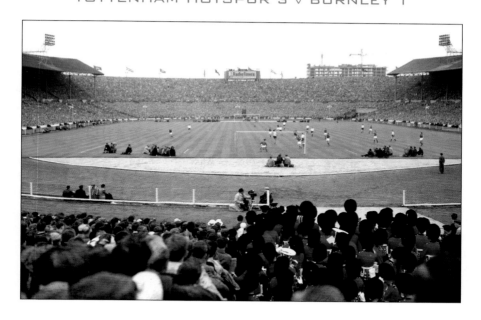

A rare colour photograph from the 1962 FA Cup final shows the incredible scene and how 100,000 fans, and a military band packed the stadium.

Bobby Smith cracks home our second goal to put us back into the lead at a crucial time in the match.

Skipper Danny Blanchflower beats Burnley goalkeeper Adam Blacklaw
to make it 3-1 from the penalty spot.

Showing off the cup with (from left)
Jimmy Greaves, Danny Blanchflower,
myself, John White and Cliff Jones.

It felt like we passed everyone in
north London on our open top
bus trip around Tottenham.

PAT JENNINGS — 1967
TOTTENHAM HOTSPUR 2 v CHELSEA 1

Manager Bill Nicholson (second left) hands out pre-match instructions to (from left) Frank Saul, Joe Kinnear, Terry Venables and myself.

Frank Saul's shot beats Peter Bonetti low to his left and we are 2-0 ahead and cruising towards a third FA Cup in six seasons.

Alan Mullery flies in with a header to beat Wolves goalkeeper Phil Parkes
and open the second leg scoring at White Hart Lane with a goal to put us
3-1 ahead on aggregate in the UEFA Cup final.

Skipper Alan Mullery holds on to the UEFA Cup as he's carried shoulder-
high by Mike England (third left) and Pat Jennings (fourth right).
Also celebrating victory are (left to right) Ralph Coates, Alan Gilzean,
Martin Peters, Joe Kinnear, Cyril Knowles and Martin Chivers.

Captaining Spurs at Wembley was one of the proudest moments
of my career, though it wasn't a great game. Here I take on
Norwich centre-half Max Briggs.

The ball is in the Norwich net, beating the despairing dive of goalkeeper
Kevin Keelan, and Ralph Coates is off across the Wembley turf on that
oft-repeated goal celebration.

Ralph celebrates the victory with his young son.

Parading the silverware around Wembley with the legendary
Cyril Knowles (right) – nice one!

GARTH CROOKS – 1981

TOTTENHAM HOTSPUR 3 v WOLVES 0

The year ends in 1, so the Cockerels will surely return to Wembley. Here the White Hart Lane groundsman tries to net a stray bird before the FA Cup quarter-final with Exeter.

Willie Carr scores the last minute equaliser in the first game. That's *Sky Sports'* Andy Gray crouched on the left in the background, unable to watch!

Skipping past Manchester City's Nicky Reid at Wembley,
We all played much better in the replay

OSSIE ARDILES &
RICKY VILLA – 1981
TOTTENHAM HOTSPUR 3 v MANCHESTER CITY 2

Ricky: My mazy run ended with me slipping the ball under
Manchester City goalkeeper Joe Corrigan...

...and racing off to celebrate a fantastic goal!

All together now... Ossie's going to Wembley,
his knees have gone all trembley!

Thousands and thousands of people waited outside Tottenham Town Hall
for us the day after we had won the Cup. It was an incredible sight!

Flying winger Tony Galvin takes on the Barcelona defence in the first leg. My goal gave us a great chance of reaching the final, but we lost narrowly in the Nou Camp.

I gave everything I had in each game I played for Spurs.

TONY PARKS — 1984
TOTTENHAM HOTSPUR 1 v ANDERLECHT 1

Graham Roberts scores the late equaliser and we're headed
for penalties and my date with destiny.

Manager Keith Burkinshaw gives me a big hug to celebrate victory.

About to put away one of my three goals against West Ham in the last ten minutes of the game, with Alvin Martin (right) just too late to stop me.

Celebrating my opening goal in the first leg of the semi-final against Arsenal. We led three times in the tie, but eventually lost in a replay.

Managers Brian Clough and Terry Venables set the friendly tone
by walking out hand in hand before the final.

Gazza lies on the Wembley turf in agony after that terrible challenge
on Gary Charles, but we couldn't let his loss affect us.

The two pivotal moments in the game. At first I thought our luck wasn't in when Mark Crossley saved Gary Lineker's penalty (left), but when Des Walker headed a corner into his own net, I felt it balanced up things after my desperately unlucky own goal which cost us the 1987 FA Cup final.

There's no better feeling than winning the FA Cup!

I was already pleased with my game in general that night, but now everything flowed. Like I said, it was just one of those nights where you're really at it and now my confidence was really high. I'd forgotten about this, but when I watched it back on tape, the crowd started singing my name after the first goal and I really seemed to feed on it.

We continued to bombard them with crosses. Knowlesy in particular was getting a lot of joy down our left and Big Chiv, Gilly and Mike England all went close before half time, all with headers.

We were really in the ascendancy now and didn't really want the half-time whistle to blow. The message from Bill was simple: more of the same and the goals will come.

As we came out for the second half the crowd started singing my name again and they were soon chanting "La la la Mullery" after Mullers put in a couple of strong challenges. The game was getting niggly now and, although they were more cynical with things like timewasting and shirt-pulling, I don't think we were entirely without blame. We certainly had plenty of players who could mix it.

I had a volley from outside the box that went just over the bar, then we should have had a penalty when Gilly was brought down, but the ref gave a free-kick just outside the box. Sogliano was booked for not retreating quickly enough and when he complained, the ref finally lost his patience and sent him off.

I'll remember the second goal to my dying day. Sabatini cleared Alan Mullery's corner to the edge of the box where I was waiting. It seemed to take an age to get to me, but I controlled it instantly and from about 22 yards struck it perfectly right into the corner on the bounce. It was an even better goal than the first one and even more important, because it changed the whole complexion of the tie.

We continued to push forward and, with only ten men, they seemed quite happy to sit back. They were happy to take 2-1 at this stage and with the away goal, they fancied their chances of getting a 1-0 in the San Siro. The Italians specialised in one-nils. In fact, they were probably happier with the result at the final whistle than we were. It's funny, because, although scoring two goals was special for me, it wouldn't have meant so much if we hadn't finished the job and at this stage, the job was only half done.

For the return leg, Bill arranged for us to stay at Inter Milan's magnificent training complex. It had a cinema, a restaurant, a hotel – it was a different world compared to what we were used, almost like being on holiday – and all the staff treated me like a king because I was the man who had scored the two goals that beat their biggest rivals. It was clever move by Bill, because it made us feel so good going into the game.

The second leg, at the old San Siro stadium, was almost as dramatic as the first, and the performance was even better – probably the best in Europe during my time at the club – because it was away from home in such a hostile environment. The San Siro was like a cauldron of hate. The height of the stands, the flares, the noise… and when we arrived at the ground the Milan fans were whacking the side of the bus with tree branches.

An early goal definitely helped and this time it was Mullers who took the mantle. I fed him 20 yards out and he curled one right into the top corner. In fact, if you think about it, the standard of goals in that tie was amazing. From that point on, we were in control. They equalised through a harshly-awarded penalty 20 minutes from time, but there were very few scares and we looked just as threatening as them going forward. The game finishd 1-1 and we went through 3-2 on aggregate to our first European final.

We'd already beaten Wolves 4-1 in the league earlier in the season, so we were confident of beating them in the final, but to be honest, we would rather have played Ferencvaros, Wolves' semi-final opponents. It would arguably have been a more difficult game, but when you play in Europe, you want to play European opposition. The element of the unknown was part of the excitement.

After winning 2-1 at Molineux, we were strong favourites going into the second leg and when Mullers headed us in front after half an hour, we thought we had it sewn up. He actually knocked himself out on the post after scoring the goal, but when he came round he just carried on playing. People joke that back then you only came off if your leg was hanging off in those days, but it isn't far from the truth.

Having attacked for most of the first-half, Wolves' equaliser just before half-time made us go into our shell a bit. After looking in complete control and threatening to run away with it, we now sat back inviting the pressure, but they didn't quite have the quality to break us down and Pat Jennings was rarely troubled in goal. The following season we beat Wolves in the League Cup semi-finals, again over two legs, and in 1981 we beat them in the semi-final of the FA Cup, after they took us to a replay. They must have been sick of the sight of us!

Two years after beating Wolves to lift the trophy, we were the ones on the losing side in the UEFA Cup Final, going down to Feyenoord 2-4 on aggregate in the final at a time when Dutch football was really coming into its own, with Ajax having just completed a hat-trick of European Cup final victories and the Dutch national side being edged out in the final of that summer's World Cup. We also lost on away goals to Liverpool after the tie finished 2-2 on aggregate in the 1972/73 semi-final. Two finals and a semi-final in three seasons – that's some record if you think about it, especially when you consider that a lot of people said the UEFA Cup was harder to win than the European Cup in those days because it contained teams who were on the up, rather thann those who had reached their peak in winning their domestic title and could well be on the way down.

We were only an upper mid-table team in the First Division during those years, but for some reason we were a different class in Europe. There was no particular change of system or tactics for European games, but things like near-post corners and overlapping full-backs, which were a given in English football, took a lot of foreign teams by surprise. We also had Martin Chivers' long throw, with big Mike England coming up from the back, and teams just couldn't cope with that.

I also think our British 'never say die' attitude helped. English teams would always go the distance. One game against Red Star Belgrade, we barely got a touch for the first few minutes. Our crowd were even applauding them. Their two star players, Karazi and Acimovic, were running the show, but after a while Pratty kicked one of them and I caught the other and they didn't fancy it after that and we won 2-0.

As for away games, when you've been to Leeds and suffered that level of hate one week, you'll have no problems with a trip to Bucharest the next.

I always thought of foreign players as being better than us somehow. They looked more elegant in the way they moved and I even thought they wore better kits than us. When I first played in Europe, I used to watch opponents as they warmed up and I remember thinking how magnificent they looked. When it game to the crunch, though, they were nowhere near as good as us.

Milan, though, they were as good as they looked, and I'm very proud to say I scored the goals that helped beat them and win the 1972 UEFA Cup for Spurs.

MARTIN PETERS
MIDFIELD 1970–1975

BORN   8 November 1943, Plaistow, London
SIGNED   March 1970 from West Ham United; £200,000
SPURS CAREER   260 games, 76 goals
HONOURS   League Cup winner 1971 & 1973, UEFA Cup winner 1972
LEFT   Transferred to Norwich City, March 1975; £60,000

Nicknamed 'The Ghost' because of his innate ability to drift through opposing defenders almost unnoticed, midfielder and Spurs captain, Martin Peters first came to prominence in Sir Alf Ramsey's World Cup winning side in 1966. As part of an ascendant West Ham triumvirate within the England ranks – the other two being defender and captain, Bobby Moore and hat-trick hero, Geoff Hurst – Peters was soon coveted by the First Division's bigger clubs, despite being overshadowed by his peers. A record breaking £200,000 transfer to White Hart Lane (which included the transfer of fans' favourite Jimmy Greaves the other way) took place in 1970. What followed was a successful tryst with Bill Nicholson's cup hungry team of the early 1970s.

Tottenham Hotspur 1 v Norwich City 0

League Cup Final
Saturday 3 March 1973

Wembley Stadium
Attendance 100,000

England's 'other' World Cup final goalscorer walks up to the Royal Box
again, only this time as a League Cup winning captain

Teams

Bill Nicholson	**Managers**	Ron Saunders
Pat Jennings	1	Kevin Keelan
Joe Kinnear	2	Clive Payne
Cyril Knowles	3	Geoff Butler
John Pratt	4	David Stringer
(Sub. Ralph Coates)		
Mike England	5	Duncan Forbes
Phil Beale	6	Max Briggs
Alan Gilzean	7	Doug Livermore
Steve Perryman	8	James Blair
		(Sub. Trevor Howard)
Martin Chivers	9	David Cross
Martin Peters	10	Graham Paddon
Jimmy Pearce	11	Terry Anderson

Coates 84	**Scorer**	

Referee: D Smith

BELIEVE ME it's a great honour to captain Tottenham Hotspur Football Club. But it carries a great pressure as well. If the team is not really playing particularly well, not performing, then you feel the pressure more than the other players in the side. Likewise, if the team's successful and winning competitions, then you get to go up and collect the trophies, like I did when I captained the team that won the League Cup in 1973.

As a performance, though, it wasn't my best game. I scored four goals in one game against Manchester United at Old Trafford in 1972/73, which was obviously a huge personal highlight and one match that people always remind me of. But the most eventful moment of my Spurs career has to be that League Cup Final. The United performance was my most outstanding game in terms of goals and individual success, but captaining the Spurs side that won the League Cup was the highlight. And walking out onto the Wembley pitch and leading the Spurs team out to play in a Cup final? Well, that's fantastic too.

You step out in front of ten other internationals, but you're the leader of the pack. You're the first person the supporters see. The expectations are high and the fans are desperate for you to win. I remember walking out with the England team in the World Cup Final in 1966, but that time I was halfway down the line and I was only 22 years-old.

By the time the League Cup Final came around I was 29, so I was a lot more experienced. I guess you could say I was naive as a player with West Ham and England in 1966, but I'd come on a lot while I was at Spurs. I was used to being one of the lads and I was part and parcel of a very good Spurs side. It was a different type of glory.

This time I was walking on to that Wembley pitch with responsibility on my shoulders, because there were tactical duties to being a Spurs captain, too. In those days the manager, Bill Nicholson, didn't stand on the sidelines barking orders. He sat on the edge of the bench, watching the game unfold, and that was it. Before the game and during half time team talks he would give us detailed instructions and expect us to carry out those orders to the letter out on the pitch and I, as his captain, was responsible for that.

That meant I would have to organise things on the pitch and this was another added pressure. You also had to gee people up. You constantly had to ensure that your players were OK and on top of their game. But I hardly ever needed to do that during my time at Tottenham. Most of the players at White Hart Lane – Alan Gilzean, Martin Chivers, Pat Jennings, Joe Kinnear, Ralph Coates – were experienced in domestic competitions and European games. A lot of them were seasoned internationals too. They all wanted to win as much as everyone else did.

But, of course, there were perks to being a captain: I walked up those 39 Wembley steps to pick up a World Cup winner's medal in 1966, but getting the League Cup trophy in 1973 – after beating Norwich City 1-0 – with Tottenham Hotspur was different, because that time I was walking up there first. I remember walking along the parapet and lifting up the trophy in front of our fans to a massive roar – it was an amazing experience. Anyone who's done the same will tell you it's a feeling you just can't put into words.

I suppose the best way to describe it was as a boyhood dream come true. Obviously the real glory – the real Roy Of The Rovers stuff – comes in the FA Cup. But in those days, the League Cup was just as exciting. And it meant another day out at Wembley. It was also important in those days because it would get a team into Europe. It might not be considered a serious trophy by some of the bigger clubs in the Premiership these days, but in the 1970s it was something to play for.

So, in hindsight, the League Cup final was a funny game because we didn't play particularly well, but we won and so we qualified for Europe the following season, which was always important for a club like Tottenham. And it kept Bill Nicholson happy.

I remember the match wasn't entertaining in the slightest, which annoyed Bill because he liked his teams to win in style. I remember there was a famous story about Bill when Spurs clinched the double in 1961. After winning the FA Cup final he was a little bit down because they hadn't won the trophy with class! Nevertheless, the most important thing to the club on this occasion was that we'd got back into European competition. And Spurs maintained their famous unbeaten run at Wembley.

Overall, though, it was a high point in a disappointing season. We'd lost in the UEFA Cup semi-final to Liverpool on away goals, which was a huge blow, but winning the League Cup obviously gave us a chance to compete abroad the next season. We met Liverpool six times that campaign – twice in the League, twice in the League Cup and then twice in the UEFA Cup.

We'd drawn 1-1 at Anfield in the League and beaten them 2-1 at White Hart Lane. In the League Cup we drew 1-1 at Anfield before beating them 3-1 at home. Sadly in Europe it wasn't to be – we lost 1-0 at Anfield and even though we beat them 2-1 at home (I scored both goals), they knocked us out on away goals. Sometimes it just doesn't go your way.

The run in to the final was tough, though. We played Wolves in the semi which was always a big match. We'd beaten them in the UEFA Cup Final the year before. It was the first time two English teams had met at that stage of the competition. In the first leg Martin Chivers scored two goals at Molineux to put us 2-1 up – he scored one goal from about 30 yards out that flew into the back of the net. Alan Mullery scored our goal in a 1-1 draw in the second, decisive leg at the Lane, and as captain he picked up the trophy for us that night.

So the two teams had history together. Given that we knew them pretty well, we beat them 2-1 at home in the League Cup semi final and I scored. Then we drew 2-2 at Molineux and I weighed in with another goal. Wolves were a good side in those days with the likes of John Richards, Mike Bailey and Kenny Hibbitt and had to be taken seriously. The semis were two great games, especially for us because our 4-3 aggregate win meant we were back at Wembley again.

I remember before those two matches, the media built the semi-final up into some sort of revenge match for Wolves, but we didn't let any of that affect us. There was obviously a lot of speculation that it was Wolves' turn to get one over on us because we weren't doing so well in the League at that time – I think we finished in fifth or sixth – but we weren't ones to pay any attention to it. And the media in those days was no way near as bad or intense as it is today.

We were confident in our ability and that was proven by the results: in both cup ties – the UEFA Cup and the League Cup – we beat Wolves away and then drew at home. It was weird. We couldn't beat them at home, but we always did well at Molineux.

Once we'd reached Wembley, we were excited. I don't think there's anything better than playing there. I've been there on a number of occasions with England, the most notable being the 1966 World Cup final. But going there with your club is just as exciting. By 1973, I'd played there quite a lot. My first game there was in 1959 as an England schoolboy and the next was the Cup Winner's Cup final in 1965 with West Ham and then came the World Cup when we played all our games there. So I have some very happy memories of that ground – the steps, the twin towers, the tunnel... it's a special place.

You always looked forward to playing at that ground, no matter how many times you'd competed there – sometimes it felt like a second home to me. I played 67 times for England, so if you take an average of 50% home games, that's quite a few matches on that famous pitch. It was a great stadium to go and play in. And of course, it was everyone's dream to play at Wembley, no matter how old you were.

I remember as a schoolboy watching the FA Cup finals – the Bert Trautman final, the Stanley Matthews final – and it was a fantastic place to look at, even on the television, let alone playing there. The place was steeped in history as well. Of course that goes back to 1923 when West Ham and Bolton played the first game there and the famous white horse was roaming around keeping the enormous crowds under control. And then I vividly remember watching the 1953 Cup final with Stanley Matthews running amok on the wing and falling in love with the place.

But we were confident we could win another trophy there. Prior to this final we'd won the League Cup in 1971 – we didn't play very well in that game against Aston Villa either, but we still managed to win 2-0 – and the UEFA Cup the previous year. We believed in ourselves. Norwich were in the First Division in those days, but they were struggling a little bit. But even so, we knew it would be a tough game. When you go to Wembley, every player raises their game and the Norwich players would be no exception. They would be up for it.

It showed on the day too. While we'd played some entertaining football throughout the season, the actual League Cup final was an anti climax. We just couldn't get our game together. Obviously we played well enough to win, but we didn't perform with our usual style against Norwich, a club I would later go on to sign for – for £60,000 – in 1975 and play for until five years later. They were a very defensive team and on that day they sat back behind the ball for long periods of the game. We really struggled to break them down early on, but once we did, we knew the cup was ours.

The opposition had got their on merit and fancied their chances – even though they were in the lower reaches of the First Division and we were in the top half. They were still a good side and had to be taken seriously. They had some top footballers, who I ended up playing alongside when I went there a couple of years later. Players like Dave Stringer, Kevin Keelan in goal, it was a pretty good team, so they had every reason to be confident, especially in a Cup final when anything can happen.

Maybe we were over confident, which was why it wasn't such a pretty game. It was scrappy stuff. Norwich put everyone behind the ball for most of the game and defended hard. We struggled to break them down, but the turning point came when John Pratt went off and winger Ralph Coates came on – he scored the winning goal and we only won one-nil. It was always nice to win at Wembley and play well. Sadly, we only did half the job and didn't do it with a flourish.

Before the game Bill sent us out there saying, "Play the way you always play." We always tried to play stylish football because we had some very attack-minded players – Martin Chivers, Alan Gilzean... I used to pop up with goals. We had a pretty sound defence too – especially with Pat Jennings in goal, who was a fantastic keeper. With players of that quality we achieved quite a lot in the early 1970s and Bill wanted us to play with flair. Sadly we didn't make the ultimate goal of winning the League or the FA Cup, but we had a strong starting XI nevertheless.

Despite our strength, I was nervous before the game, but then I was always nervous before any match. Most players are. Obviously with it being a Cup final, you're a lot more edgy than normal and if you don't get nervous, you haven't got the right attitude.

Whatever game you play, whether it's a White Hart Lane, Wembley or wherever, you need to get nervous because you need to build yourself up. Especially at Tottenham, where expectations were always high. You wanted to go out there and prove you were as good as everyone else in the League.

The mood in the dressing room was good. We were pumped up and up for it. We had a lot of piss-takers in the squad at the time – Phil Beale, Terry Naylor, Joe Kinnear – so there was a laugh going on, but when it got to the last half an hour before the game it got serious. You had to behave because Bill was around, as was assistant coach, Eddie Baily, who was a strict disciplinarian. He would get upset with a few of the players every now and then and give his opinion quite strongly. We'd listen and take it in, but when Bill said it, you knew that he meant it.

Bill was actually very similar to [World Cup winning England manager] Alf Ramsey. Their expectations were very high and the players respected them. If they asked you to do something, you knew you had to do it.

They came out from the same mould, they both played for Spurs, and I could see the similarities between the two. With the team talk done, we moved into the tunnel. I remember the roar as we walked into the daylight and out on to the pitch.

The crowd is always great at Wembley and both sides of supporters were well behaved, but I remember the ground being split between yellow and white – it looked fantastic. And the noise was amazing. It made for a great atmosphere . Our fans wanted another trophy and Norwich didn't really go to Wembley that often, so it was a massive day out for them. We'd been there two years previously and Spurs fans almost expected to get to Cup finals in those days. We were such a successful Cup team through history. I had a good relationship with the White Hart Lane crowd, although I remember it was difficult at first because I replaced Jimmy Greaves in a part exchange with West Ham. It was difficult to settle because Jimmy was such a favourite with the Spurs fans. He was a terrific striker and he'd scored a lot of goals for Tottenham. In the first quarter of the season it was very hard for me to bed in, especially once Jimmy started scoring a lot of goals for West Ham. He scored on his debut – which I believe he did at every club he played for. I scored on my debut and scored one more in the next ten games, and I was gradually accepted, especially once the team started playing well. It helped that, suddenly, West Ham weren't doing so well. It didn't take long before I'd managed to win the fans over.

The thing was, I was never a Jimmy Greaves and Greavesie was never a Martin Peters. And the expectations for new players at a club like Spurs was very, very high, even then. So if you had a blip of maybe two or three games where you hadn't won or played well, then the supporters would soon be on your back. That has definitely changed at White Hart Lane.

In those days it was difficult because, at Spurs, the fans wanted the team to play with style and flair and score a lot of goals and win games. It was the same at West Ham. But I remember at both clubs playing really well and losing in League matches and everyone going home unhappy, so you have to strike a balance. Saying that, West Ham won seven-nil once against Leeds, six-nil against Fulham, we drew five-all with Chelsea, and we lost five-four to Leicester. The thing was, we played cracking football, but we weren't consistent with the results. Good football is very difficult to attain if you want to get results all the time.

I think Bill Nicholson got the balance right at Spurs in the early 70s. We were great at playing attractive football and we were winning trophies as well – though sadly not the FA Cup or the First Division title. But we did well in Europe – we lost in the final of the UEFA cup in 1974 and we lost a couple of semis as well as our victory in 1972. But we just couldn't crack it in the League. I remember we came third in 1970/71, but that was the highest we finished while I was there.

We knew the cups were our strong point, and once we started the League Cup final in 1973, we realised that Norwich had set out to stifle us rather than play their own game. They did it very well too. Ron Saunders was the manager then. Had John Bond been in charge, they would have played very differently because he liked attacking football.

It only took one goal to finish them off, but it's one I'll never forget, simply because I was involved and Ralph Coates rounded it off with a now legendary celebration.

There was a throw in deep the Norwich half. We always practiced those moves: Martin Chivers always used to hurl the ball into the near post and strangely enough the ball used to go to Alan Gilzean, but this time it came to me and I flicked it on. The ball dropped on the edge of the box and Ralphy came in and it hit it with a first time volley. It screamed into the far corner past the keeper, then, before we knew it, he was on his run around Wembley waving his arms around. They still show his celebration on the pre-match video that they play on the big screens at White Hart Lane before Premiership games. It was a great celebration and the goal was good enough for us to win the cup.

I played OK that day, though I remember playing a lot better in a lot of other games. But that doesn't matter when you lift that trophy in front of 100,000 odd people. It's a weird sensation. People pat you on the back as you climb the 39 stairs, shout "Congratulations!", but you're in a world of your own and you can't really hear what individuals are saying.

It's more a case of one big noise. It's the same as you come down the other side, though you have to be careful when you're walking in your football boots. You don't want to skid on your studs and have a nasty fall. There's a famous picture of Jack Charlton falling down them after he had collected his medal at the World Cup final.

Winning trophies is weird – you take those experiences one stage at a time. I remember it was an amazing experience playing in the World Cup final, but you have to take every game as it comes. Our next game was against Czechoslovakia in a friendly at Wembley, which was just as exciting. The attitude is the same for every game: you want to go out there, win and play well. And you can't beat being the best team in the world, can you?

Undoubtedly, England were the best team in the world at that time. We'd won the biggest competition in global football. But once you get back to your club you want to do as well as you can. When I moved from West Ham to Spurs the desire to win things was just as strong, but I probably had more pressure on me when I went to White Hart Lane because I was the highest transfer fee in England at the time. I guess Jimmy Greaves had the same pressure going to West Ham, so we all experienced it at one stage or another. But, in general, there was a lot of pressure on me in the 1970s, but luckily I managed to play well in Bill Nicholson's Tottenham side. I scored quite a few goals along the way and we won some trophies which pleased the fans. Even better, I built up a cracking relationship on the football field with some fantastic players like Martin Chivers. I had a great time at Spurs. When Bill Nicholson was there, I seriously believed I'd stay at White Hart Lane until the end of my career.

Bill was always happy if we won something. He wasn't very happy about the way we played on that afternoon at Wembley in 1973, because it wasn't the prettiest to look at, but at the end of the day winning anything is not just about one game, it's about a multitude of matches. Each one is just as important because it gets you through the tournament and one step closer to victory.

After the League Cup final the mood in the dressing room was amazing. The champagne was flying around. We poured it into the trophy and every-body was in a fantastic mood. Not only had we grabbed a cup at Wembley, but we were back in Europe. Afterwards we went to a big function in the Grosvenor House Hotel to celebrate. Bill was happy for you to let your hair down after games like that – certainly you were allowed to relax more. I had to say a few words at the dinner because I was the captain – I can't remember what I said, but that was even more pressure! Certainly I speak a lot better today than I did then. I was never any good at speaking in front of an audience.

Looking back, that's quite funny, because these days I'm involved with the match day hospitality at White Hart Lane. There's eight former players involved including Cliff Jones, Paul Allen, Pat Jennings, Ralphy Coates, Alan Mullery and Phil Beale – a lot of players who I worked with. We all have our lounges to look after and it's great fun meeting the fans before a game. It's a great day, the ground is fantastic, but it could do with being bigger. White Hart Lane holds 36,000 these days, which isn't enough. It's sold out all the time, but when I played, it used to hold 60,000 fans on some matches, especially for the big cup games. Of course, the supporters were standing on the old terraces, but I believe Tottenham might have to think seriously about relocating or building a new ground. Like Arsenal have done, I guess. It's been on the agenda for a long time now because they're attracting 36,000 fans every game when they could be attracting 46,000.

Winning at Wembley was a high, though. I left Spurs a couple of years later and moved to Norwich City. It was another step in my career. Bill Nicholson had resigned by then and Terry Neill had taken over his position as manager. I had a hard three quarters of a season with Terry Neill and I didn't get on with him, as did a lot of the players who'd played under Bill Nick. And I had the offer to go to Norwich City and I decided to take it. Like I said, I actually thought that I would be at Tottenham for the rest of my life, especially with Bill as manager, but things change very quickly in football and I was off to Carrow Road.

I have to say that, although it was a different scenario at Norwich, I enjoyed the five and a half years I had there immensely. I had a great time at Tottenham though, and there were so many highlights. Winning the UEFA Cup against Wolves was brilliant and winning three cups in three years (two League Cups in 1971 and 73 and the UEFA Cup) has to be considered as pretty good business.

So was scoring those four goals against Manchester United. What a game. Bill had decided to play me up front in Alan Gilzean's position. I'm not sure why – maybe Gilly was injured – but I wasn't good enough to play up front because I wasn't quick enough, but it happened for me that day. The ball seemed to stick to my feet and I put four away. That was in the 1972/73 season, an era when Manchester United were struggling, but because it happened at Old Trafford that still made it a pretty special game.

Throughout my Tottenham career, I played with some great players – Martin Chivers was the best centre-forward in Europe for the five years I was there; Pat Jennings was the best goalkeeper in the world after Gordon Banks damaged his eye in 1972. If you've got those two in your line-up, you've got half a chance against any team in the world. But the whole squad was fantastic. We were a unit. We were one of those sides that went out together. We got drunk together and relaxed together. That meant we fought for each other.

On our day we could outplay anyone, especially in the cup competitions. And in those days, winning trophies was a Spurs speciality.

GARTH CROOKS
STRIKER 1980–1985

BORN   10 March 1958, Stoke-on-Trent
SIGNED   June 1980 from Stoke City; £650,000
SPURS CAREER   125 appearances, 48 goals
HONOURS   FA Cup Winner 1981, 1982
LEFT   Free transfer to West Bromwich Albion, August 1985

A sharp turn of pace and keen eye for goal were the qualities that persuaded Keith Burkinshaw to bring Garth Crooks to White Hart Lane in the summer of 1980. Crooks began repaying the £650,000 transfer fee with four goals in his first three games and soon formed a fruitful partnership with fellow new recruit Steve Archibald. Though 1981 will forever be remembered for Ricky Villa's stunning winner in the FA Cup Final replay, it was two strikes from Crooks in the semi-final replay that put Spurs on the their way to Wembley.

Tottenham Hotspur 3 v Wolverhampton Wanderers 0

FA Cup semi-final replay
Wednesday 15 April 1981

Highbury
Attendance 52,539

Lightning strikes twice as a young striker from Stoke puts Spurs on their way to Wembley

Teams

	Managers	
Keith Burkinshaw	**Managers**	John Barnwell
Milija Aleksic	1	Paul Bradshaw
Chris Hughton	2	Geoff Palmer
Paul Miller	3	Derek Parkin
Graham Roberts	4	Emlyn Hughes
		(Sub. Wayne Clarke)
Ricky Villa	5	John McAlle
Steve Perryman	6	George Berry
Ossie Ardiles	7	Kenny Hibbitt
(Sub. Gary Brooke)		
Steve Archibald	8	Willie Carr
Tony Galvin	9	Norman Bell
Glenn Hoddle	10	John Richards
Garth Crooks	11	Mel Eves

Crooks 10, 45, Villa 55   **Scorers**

Referee: C Thomas

I₁ₜ'S APT THAT MY most memorable game for Spurs should have come in an FA Cup semi-final, because one of my earliest, most vivid memories in football was of an FA Cup semi-final. In fact, I remember it like it was yesterday.

I was a 14-year-old fan in 1972 when I went to Hillsborough to watch my team Stoke City, play Arsenal, who had won the 'Double' the previous season. It was all the town spoke about for weeks leading up to the game. We'd hadn't been in an FA Cup semi-final since 1899 and there we were playing the mighty Arsenal, with all their history and all their panache.

I didn't know I was going until 24 hours before the game and when I found out I'd been given a ticket by someone at the club it was just the most magnificent moment in my teenage life. The traffic was a nightmare, and it took what seemed like ages to get into the ground – there were over 50,000 there – but it didn't matter to me. Stoke also had a good team, who had won the League Cup final against Chelsea the previous month, so, although we were underdogs, everybody thought we had a chance.

I can see John Ritchie scoring our second goal now – and there we were, 2-0 up against the Arsenal at half-time and staring at a place in the FA Cup Final. I remember thinking, "we've got one foot at Wembley" – and that's when the nightmare started...

We, and by that I mean the team, started saying to ourselves, "how are we going to close this game out?" I was thinking, "we're 2-0 up here – why are we nervous, what are we afraid of?" But you could feel the tension and the nervousness increasing, and very quickly the euphoria of being 2-0 ahead completely disappeared. We were gripped by fear. Gripped. And that fear transmitted from the players to the fans – not the other way round, as is often the case.

From playing controlled, winning football, we soon weren't in control anymore, and the fans recognised it. As the players panicked more and more, so did we. It was only when I became a professional footballer myself that I understood that from a position of strength you could be at your most vulnerable. This was a classic example.

Then Arsenal scored. Two-one. More panic. It was no longer a case of, "oh no, that was a bad ball, get it down and play!!!" Now it was, "hoof it, get it out, get it forward!!!"

Then, four minutes into injury time, Arsenal get a corner down their right-hand side. From the corner, centre-forward John Radford goes up against Gordon Banks, the greatest goalkeeper in the world, who is fouled – but the referee, Pat Partridge, doesn't give it (these days, it would definitely have been a foul). The ball comes to out to the edge of the box, Peter Storey drives it goalwards and Stoke midfielder John Mahoney, standing on the line, dives and saves it. Penalty. Arsenal equalise, the game is drawn, we lose the replay and the whole direction of the club is changed. It was a pivotal moment in my young life – as a fan and as a player – and one I'll never forget.

The next time I'm at Hillsborough is nine years later, almost to the day, and I'm lining up for Spurs, Arsenal's great rivals, in the semi-final of the FA Cup against Wolves. It was the replay four days later that holds the fondest memories for me, though that year will forever be remembered for our two dramatic matches against Manchester City in the final, and a spectacular winner by Ricky Villa in the replay – a game in which I also scored.

How many people remember that I scored the two goals that put us into the final? I don't care. I remember, you remember, the Spurs fans remember. I can see why people might think Ricky stole my thunder, but I don't see it that way. I'm just pleased to have played my part in something special and it's there in the record books – FA Cup semi-final replay, 1981: Crooks 2. And that's something that gives me enormous pride and pleasure.

Tottenham had always been my second team. I loved the way they played and that brand of football was something I wanted to be part of. So when I heard they wanted to sign me I couldn't believe it. It was January 1980, six months before I actually joined them, when I first knew they were interested, and that was a tortuous period for me. Once a player knows that another club is interested, and a club that's going to improve you as a player and further your career, it's very difficult to concentrate on the job in hand – your mind is already somewhere else. But I managed to get through the remainder of the season with Stoke and the deal went through in June 1980.

Even though £650,000 was a lot of money at the time, I didn't really think about the transfer fee. I just wanted to get down to London, get playing and prove to myself and to other people that I could play for a big club and win things. I'd played with Glenn Hoddle for the England under-21 team, so I knew what he was all about, and now I couldn't wait to play with the likes of Ossie Ardiles and Ricky Villa as well. My attitude was, "let's get it on!"

Steve Archibald joined from Aberdeen £800,000 around the same time. Despite all the creative talent I've just mentioned, it was felt that Spurs needed a couple of strikers who could put the ball in the net. He was a great player, Steve – a truly great striker. He had everything: pace, skill, intelligence, great touch, good in the air, and he could play whatever role you wanted him to, either with a partner or up front on his own.

We both had to change our games when we came to White Hart Lane. When I was at Stoke I played a lot of football with my back to goal, but Glenn Hoddle had such passing ability that the only time I ever faced the play was to give him the ball back. If I could position myself whereby I was facing the goal, he had the quality to put me in, which is exactly what would happen in the semi-final replay against Wolves. Steve also worked that out and that's why we scored so many goals – particularly in that first season when we got 47 between us in all competitions. It wasn't easy, though…

I was speaking to Steve recently about this, and there were times when we'd have rows with the midfield and they'd have rows with us. They felt we didn't give them the ball when they wanted it, and we felt they didn't put us in when we needed them to. Both parties were a little bit self-indulgent at times. It would be fair to say we came to some sort of arrangement: outside the box they were in charge, inside the box we were in charge – but it was only a loosely held agreement!

Could Ossie and Ricky have played for any other team in England? Probably not. Tottenham was a club that accommodated players with exceptional talent perhaps more than any other. Liverpool were THE team of my era, the dominant force, but they had talent and brawn in equal measure, whereas we had more talent than brawn. Did Keith Burkinshaw get the balance wrong? Maybe. But above all else, Spurs were expected to play in a certain way – perhaps to our detriment at times. Perhaps that way of playing was not conducive to dominating English football for a sustained period? Perhaps we should have stayed together as a team for a bit longer? We certainly should have won the league championship with the players we had, but it wasn't to be.

Going to Spurs didn't just change my football career, it changed my life – in so many different ways. It introduced me to the media, and it introduced me to the cosmopolitan metropolis that is London, that wonderful melting pot of different cultures, different people and different attitudes. Suddenly, this young lad from Stoke-on-Trent born of Jamaican immigrants found himself in a place where there were so many opportunities – and I was keen to grab as many of them as I could.

I even went back to school. I'd been in a football environment for such a long time and I was a bit concerned about what level my academic learning was at. I'd go to Tottenham Tech with my baseball cap on and my leather jacket done right up to try and make myself inconspicuous, and sit at the back of the class. People used to do double takes as if to say, "is that really him?!"

I took an English A-level and had a fantastic time with this wonderful teacher – I forget her name now – who really brought the subject life. She was so enthusiastic, so articulate and she could express herself in a way which you could understand. I was fascinated by her. Learning became fun again.

Classes were on Tuesday and she'd come in and tell you about what she'd been up to at the weekend. One time, she went to great lengths to tell us about a dinner party she had hosted, and how one guest just sat there and contributed nothing to the conversation. That really irritated her and it really stuck with me. I didn't like the idea of being the person at the dinner party who contributed nothing. If I could arm myself with the books and the tools to be able to offer an opinion and contribute to a debate, I'd be happy. That's why I went to North London University and did a degree and that's why I went to King's College and did a second degree. I don't know if I'm any better for it, mind you, but it's a time I look back upon with great fondness.

When I joined Spurs they'd only been back in Division One for two seasons after a brief flirtation with the Second Division following relegation in 1977. Although they'd only finished in mid-table since their return, expectations were high, especially as Steve Archibald and I had be brought in specifically to solve what was perceived to be their main weakness: scoring goals.

I scored on my competitive debut against Nottingham Forest, added two more against Crystal Palace three days later – both games which we won – and scored again against Brighton in a 2-2 draw to make it four in three games. That day I was up against a certain Mark Lawrenson, now my BBC colleague. He was already a great defender, Mark – he moved on to Liverpool at the end of that season – and we always got on well.

I knew after those three games that I was part of something special, but the derby at Highbury was the start of six-game goal drought for me, which coincided with a dip in form for the team and we were soon off the pace in the league. It wasn't long before I was banging in the goals again, but we never really got going in the league. Having beaten Arsenal in the previous round, we were knocked out of the League Cup by West Ham, who were then in the Second Division, in the quarter-finals, leaving the FA Cup as our only chance of silverware.

We only picked up two points from a possible six over Christmas, before heading to Loftus Road for a third round FA Cup tie against Queen's Park Rangers, who were also in the Second Division at the time. What had happened to us against West Ham in the League Cup was in the back of our minds and to be honest, we should have been beaten by QPR as well. But we managed to scrape a 0-0 draw. In the dressing room afterwards, Keith Burkinshaw turned round to us and said, "I tell you, this could be our year." Then somebody said something about Spurs winning the Cup when the year ends in '1'. I thought, "what is this superstitious nonsense?" But then I checked the record books and they were right.

And if you look at it, we had a pretty favourable run to the semi-finals. I scored as we won replay against QPR 3-1 and we were then drawn at home in the next three rounds – first against a Third Division side (Hull City), then against a struggling First Division side (Coventry City) and then, in the quarter-finals, against another Third Division side (Exeter City) – all games which we won comfortably. Of course, nobody remembers Spurs getting lucky in the third round or getting a string of home ties – they just remember Ricky Villa's winning goal. It's a rose-tinted view in retrospect, but it's the old cliché about people only remembering the winners.

It was the same the following year. The run itself was far more difficult. We beat Arsenal, Leeds United and, most memorably, Chelsea at Stamford Bridge, and I scored winning goals in three of the rounds, but all most people remember is that we beat QPR in the final replay after a couple if tight games. That's football. That's the FA Cup.

Despite Tottenham Hotspur's tremendous FA Cup pedigree, this was the club's first appearance in the semi-finals since 1967 – a game which was also played at Hillsborough – so demand for tickets was very high. As I walked out in front of 50,000 people the first thing I saw was the Spurs fans in the Leppings Lane End away to the left and I remember turning to Steve Archibald and saying, "there's a lot of people in that end – how did they get them all in? As my focus turned to the game I thought no more of it. Little did I know what events would unfold eight years later in that very same stand.

The next second, I was thinking about that semi-final against Arsenal nine years earlier and how we [Stoke] had had the game in our grasp – and suddenly it was taken away. Lightning would nearly strike twice. Like Stoke, Spurs went ahead early. In the fourth minute, we carved open the Wolves defence, as we always had the ability to do, and Steve Archibald calmly slotted in his 25th goal of the season. Wolves dug in and hit back almost immediately, Kenny Hibbitt latching on to one of Andy Gray's trademark knock-downs and hitting it low past Milija Aleksic.

Although Wolves got back in the game and equalised very quickly, at no point did we feel under pressure in the first half. We always felt we could create the chances to win the game, so there was no tension, no nervousness. We controlled the remainder of the first half and just before the interval we got the goal we deserved. In truth, it had been coming.

Ossie got the ball and went on one of those scampering runs of his, straight towards the Wolves penalty area. George Berry slid in and brought Ossie down and his momentum took him tumbling into the penalty area. The Wolves players claimed it was a fair tackle, but it was definitely a foul – I don't think there's any doubt about that. The only issue was whether it was inside the box or not. We appealed for a penalty, of course, but Clive Thomas – no stranger to controversy as everybody knows – awarded a free-kick right on the edge of the box, inside the D.

At first we were disappointed, but then we all started to laugh – I kid you not – because we'd seen Glenn Hoddle practising free-kicks from that exact same position every day in training and he could literally place them any-where he liked. And in the week leading up to that game, not only had he been scoring every one, he'd actually been sending the keeper the wrong way, just like Eric Cantona or Matthew Le Tissier used to do from the penalty spot.

To add another twist to the incident, the last spot-kick Glenn had missed was against Paul Bradshaw, the Wolves keeper having saved one from him the previous season (although he'd also scored one against him in the league earlier in this season), so he was actually glad the infringement had occurred outside the box!

Anyway, as Steve Archibald and I went to take our positions in the penalty area we just looked at each other and burst out laughing. Then we looked across at Paul Miller and he was laughing as well. I said to Steve, "do you think he'll go for it? Do you think he'll try to send the keeper the wrong way?" Because in a game like that it's easy to play it safe, bottle it if you like, rather than try something different, something he'd been doing on the training ground all week. We tried to stop laughing and took up our positions as normal, so as to not alert the Wolves players that something out of the ordinary might be happening.

Glenn placed the ball down, then he had this nervous routine whereby he would stub the toes on his right foot into the ground, a kind of mental preparation he would go through as the opposition were lining up the wall. He waited for all the usual pre-free-kick commotion to die down, waited for Clive Thomas to blow his whistle, then looked into one top corner and put it in the other! HA HA HA!!! We couldn't believe it – we were laughing all the way back to the centre-circle. In those pressure situations it's very easy to look foolish if you try something like that and it doesn't come off, but that was the measure of Glenn Hoddle the player.

At 2-1 up, we were confident of seeing the game out – unlike Stoke in 1972 – and Keith Burkinshaw told us to keep it going. With just one goal in it, it was nip and tuck all the way, and Wolves threw everything at us, but we always looked comfortable. Then came a twist…

Kenny Hibbitt gets the ball, goes into the box and takes a chance, going to ground under Glenn Hoddle's tackle, which looks clean at first glance. As Hibbitt lies on the ground pointing to the spot, we all look at Clive Thomas for what seems like an age. He looks at it, and looks it, before deciding it's a penalty. We remonstrate – I remember Ossie and Steve getting particularly irate – but to no avail. Willie Carr scores the equaliser and the game goes into extra-time. But both sets of players are utterly drained and it finishes 2-2.

People might find it odd that Glenn was the one making the last-ditch tackle, but it wasn't as unusual as you might think. Look at the FA Cup final replay against Manchester City – I can recall him making a number of tackles that day. He wasn't the greatest tackler in the world, but he wasn't afraid to put his foot in. I thought he got that particular tackle at Hillsborough right and to add insult to injury, the television replays proved me correct. In fact, it looks like Kenny Hibbitt dived, but that was academic now – we were heading for a replay.

All things being equal, we were confident of getting a result. As it turned out, things weren't quite equal. There had, it transpired, been a severe crush in the Leppings Lane End during the first game, forcing South Yorkshire Police to move a number of Spurs fans into the Kop End, where there was more room. The Spurs fans should really have been allocated that end in the first place.

To avoid a repeat of the incident, the replay was switched to Highbury, which of course, was just up the road for us, and this time the Spurs fans seriously outnumbered their Wolves counterparts. We felt there was a certain injustice about what had happened right at the end of normal time at Hillsborough, so we weren't complaining. But I think the suggestion that we were at an advantage because we only had to travel down the road holds true. It was like a home game for us, which was strange given that it was played at the home of our biggest rivals.

With the Highbury pitch immaculate as usual, we were sure that if we played our football and kept our concentration, we would win the game, so Keith Burkinshaw's messages before the game were fairly simple. Then we received the news that Andy Gray, who had battled his way through the first game, had failed a late fitness test and wouldn't even be on the bench. That was a massive boost to us. Massive. Wolves were going to be without their star player and main goal threat. You can't underestimate the boost that gave us. Now everything was in our favour.

The other thing about Andy was, you knew if he was playing the game was going to be a full-on battle for 90 minutes. I remember Emlyn Hughes saying to me that Andy was one of these players that, if he didn't come off the pitch with six stitches in his head, he hadn't had a good game! That bravery alone put the fear of God into defenders. He'd get smashed in the head, broken cheekbones, cuts above the eyebrow. He put his body in positions that asked questions of defenders. Either you pulled your own head out of the way and gave him a clear header at goal, or you went in there where it hurt.

And, of course, there was the suggestion that if there was one thing Spurs lacked, it was grit – the stomach for the fight. You had to earn the right to play the style of football we wanted to play and we didn't always do that. You can't always just go out and play, because some teams won't let you. They'll deny you space, make it difficult for you, and if you try to play as normal before you've won the battle, you'll come unstuck. I suppose in some respects we were arrogant about playing 'our way' as opposed to lacking grit. We could scrap and battle if we wanted to. You could never accuse the likes of Steve Perryman, Graham Roberts and Paul Miller of not being up for the fight. The best example is the 1981 FA Cup Final replay, where we really had to dig in deep.

I remember walking out with the team at Highbury for the semi-fnal replay as if it was yesterday. It was a spring night, perfect for football, and we were all in white, which was a rarity for us. It was one of those evening cup ties that had a certain buzz about it – it was terrific. I can't explain it, but sometimes you just feel like it's going to be your night and that was certainly one of those occasions.

We played well – some of the Spurs fans even joked it had been the best performance by the home team at Highbury all season! But Wolves certainly weren't the same side we had faced at Hillsborough four days earlier. That day they were in your faces, never giving you an inch, battling for everything. In the replay I think they felt a little bit intimidated. Maybe it was because they were a lot further from home than us, maybe it was Andy Gray's absence, maybe they'd had their big chance at Hillsborough and hadn't taken it.

Fired up by what had happened in the first game, we started well. Glenn Hoddle received the ball from a throw-in on the right and with his first touch, just helped it on towards the penalty box. The ball loops into the air towards George Berry and as he goes to meet it, suddenly I realise he's not going to get to the pitch of the ball. The ball bounces over his head – and he had some hair in those days! – and at that point I know I'm quick enough to get there. What I wasn't quite sure of was where goalkeeper Paul Bradshaw was. When the ball went over George Berry, I thought he might leave his six-yard box, come and meet it at the top of the bounce and punch it out. He began to come, but then, for some reason, he hesitated and suddenly found himself in no man's land. From that point onwards it was relatively easy for me – I knew exactly what I was doing. There was no need to panic, because he was in the worst possible position and I knew I would get there first. I was decent in the air for my height (5ft 8in) and I looped my header over Bradshaw into the net. It was very strange to be celebrating in front of a North Bank packed with delirious Spurs fans, but I was delighted.

Going 1-0 up so early really settled everybody down and, from that moment on, I knew that, providing we just played our natural game and everybody kept their nerve, it wouldn't be problem. Wolves came at us as we knew they would and they even hit the woodwork, but we always looked the more likely to score next – and just before half-time, we did.

My second goal was my best in the FA Cup and one of the best of my career – firstly, because of the quality of the pass, secondly because of the quality of the finish. Some reports said it was a "lightning burst" that took me away from the Wolves defenders. I don't know about that. You can teach a farmer to run, but you can't teach him to play a ball with the outside of his foot with backspin, as Glenn Hoddle did to put me in. And I don't think you can teach him to despatch it the way I did – with my weaker foot.

Not many people picked up on that. Although I was predominantly left-footed, I wasn't bad with my right. I worked hard on my weaker foot, because a wonderful old guy at Stoke called Doug Brown told me that if I didn't, it would hold me back. And I'm glad I listened to him because, if I hadn't, my FA Cup exploits would have been very different. People talk about my goal in the final and the fact that I scored a rare header against Wolves, but that second goal is my favourite. It was a great pass by a great player and I'm glad to say I did it justice. Whenever I see that goal it gives me a tremendous amount of pleasure.

I actually should have scored a hat-trick in that game. The Spurs fans were already celebrating victory when I was clean through on goal with ten minutes to go, but I laid it on for Steve Archibald instead and he fluffed it – I couldn't believe it! I don't know how many people have scored a hat-trick in an FA Cup semi-final, but I decided to square it to him for some reason – we always looked after each other like that. After he missed that chance I remember him putting his hands on his knees and then sliding them over his face as if to say, "I can't believe I just did that!" He daren't look at me.

We did get a third goal in the end, and it was that man Ricky Villa who got it. And it was another great strike, a curler from outside the box, which he made look so easy. Again, you could argue that he stole my thunder, but I didn't see it that way. I certainly wasn't thinking about that as the Spurs fans invaded the pitch at the final whistle and we headed for the tunnel before they could mob us.

It had been eight years since Spurs had been to Wembley and it was great for the supporters. For me, it was a dream come true. I'd grown up watching *FA Cup Final Grandstand*, which was always a big event, and now I was in the eye of the storm. After the semi-final, all my sights were on the final, although I nearly didn't make it. I pulled a thigh muscle against Liverpool at Anfield and missed our last two league games, but I recovered in time to play a testimonial game the Wednesday before the final and thankfully I came through unscathed.

Although I was 100 percent fit, I was battling with nerves on the day of the game. I'd seen Wembley a million times, but as the team coach made its way down Wembley Way with all the fans lining the sidewalks either side, I was getting more and more nervous with every second. That day, I deliberately stuck close to Ricky Villa – whose memories of the '81 Cup Final you will read next – because he was the coolest man I've ever come across.

Amid all the hysteria, all the madness, he was ice cold, and I was hoping some of that would rub off on me.

But when I went out on to the pitch in my suit for the pre-match walk-about – ooh, I thought my legs were going to give way. Then I saw the Spurs fans standing at the same end I stood nine years earlier when Stoke beat Chelsea to win the League Cup. At that point all my confidence came flooding back. It was quite an empowering experience to see all those fans there wanting us to do well for them. There was even a banner that said something like 'Number 11 Crooks for Number 10'. They were referring to Downing Street, of course. That made me chuckle and at that point I was ready.

OSSIE ARDILES & RICKY VILLA
MIDFIELD 1978-1988 / 1978-1983
*ARDILES CAREER STATS FIRST, FOLLOWED BY VILLA

BORN   3 June 1952, Córdoba, Argentina / 18 August 1952, Buenos Aires, Argentina
SIGNED   June 1978 / June 1978
SPURS CAREER   309 games, 25 goals / 178 games, 25 goals
HONOURS   FA Cup winner 1981 & 1982, FA Cup runner-up 1987, UEFA Cup winner 1984 / FA Cup winner 1981
LEFT   Joined Swindon Town as player-manager, July 1989 / Transferred to Fort Lauderdale Strikers, July 1982

When Argentinian superstars Ossie Ardiles and Ricky Villa arrived at White Hart Lane in a blur of World Cup ticker tape and flashbulbs in 1978, it kickstarted a foreign revolution within English football. Their arrival signalled exciting times for Tottenham too. As the pair settled, Spurs moved from the shadow of relegation into a new era based on stylish football and flair, twinned with cup success. Ardiles endeared himself with a string of performances based on skill and workrate, forging an incisive partnership with an emerging Glenn Hoddle in the Spurs midfield. Villa, meanwhile, found it harder to settle, despite scoring on his debut against Nottingham Forest (with 10,000 fans locked outside the City Ground). Though one game in May 1981 was to change his public image forever...

Tottenham Hotspur 3 v Manchester City 2

FA Cup final replay
Thursday 14 May 1981

Wembley Stadium
Attendance 92,000

Ricky Villa scores the greatest FA Cup final goal

Teams

Keith Burkinshaw	**Managers**	John Bond
Milia Aleksic	1	Joe Corrigan
Chris Hughton	2	Ray Ranson
Paul Miller	3	Bobby McDonald
Graham Roberts	4	Nicky Reid
Ricky Villa	5	Paul Power
Steve Perryman	6	Tommy Caton
Ossie Ardiles	7	Dave Bennett
Steve Archibald	8	Gerry Gow
Tony Galvin	9	Steve Mackenzie
Glenn Hoddle	10	Tommy Hutchison
Garth Crooks	11	Kevin Reeves

Villa 8, 76, Crooks 70	**Scorers**	Mackenzie 11, Reeves 50

Referee: K Hackett

IT'S RARE THAT the opportunity presents itself to learn the memories of both of Spurs' Argentinian heroes, Ossie Ardiles and Ricky Villa about that incredible 1981 FA Cup Final replay against Manchester City. This exclusive interview was conducted on one of the few occasions that the pair have both been simultaneously in the UK since their playing days ended.

RICKY: Scoring the winning goal in the 1981 FA Cup final was the most wonderful goal of my life. I guess it's the sort of goal you dream about scoring: the FA Cup final decider, especially when it's an individual goal where you dribble around a few defenders and tuck it past the keeper. Even now, I look back and feel lucky to have scored such a great goal, because it's a goal I tried to score all my life and I never managed to do it ever again.

Today, it's one of the moments in FA Cup history that people always talk about. I can't believe that 25 years on from that goal, people – some of them Spurs fans, some of them fans of other clubs – still want to talk to me about it. It's important to so many people. I'm so proud to be part of English football history.

OSSIE: And we were playing at Wembley too. It was an amazing stadium to play in. After that match I played there a few times – in the League Cup final the following season and in the FA Cup final in 1982 and in 1987, but that was the best time. It's the Cup final that stuck out in my mind. Before the game we actually recorded a single with (Cockney duo and Spurs fans) Chas'n'Dave. We all went into the studio and that's when I realised they had called the single, *Ossie's Dream*, with the lyrics "Ossie's going to Wembley/ His knees have gone all trembley". Before the game everything was focused on the Spurs point of view, not just me. But I had been saying how much I wanted to play at Wembley and play well and how it was my dream to play there because there was so much history. Suddenly before the game the focus became on me and not Ricky. I didn't want to do the single though. I didn't like the lyric "In the cup for Tott-ing-ham". A lot was made of the way I said Tottenham and I didn't like it. I didn't want to do the line, but after a few beers and some encouragement from all the boys I went along with it.

RICKY: Although the mood was expectant before the game, it could have been so different once we got on the pitch. We played the first game against Manchester City and it was a 1-1 draw after extra time, which was a shame because it was meant to be such a special occasion. It was the 100th FA Cup final after all. Despite the build up, the game was quite boring and we didn't play as well as we could have done. In fact, I remember the first game was very difficult for me to play in and I didn't do very well at all. I played so badly that Keith Burkinshaw took me off, which was a real disappointment for me. I had to accept that decision, despite the fact that it was an FA Cup final. In some games you can play well, in others you can play badly. It was my turn to play badly. I'd played quite well all season, but on the big day it wasn't meant to be; which is why I prefer talking about the second game – the replay six days later.

But what I did love about the first game was the experience of playing at Wembley. It was great. It's the home of football. The fans are fantastically loud and there's so much colour. As soon as Ossie and I arrived in England from Argentina in 1978, we knew we had to play at Wembley and it was what every fan and player talked about all the time. In Argentina we knew bits about the FA Cup, but once we arrived everybody was talking about the FA Cup and what it meant to Spurs. We soon came to understand it's importance and I decided that even if it was only once, I had to play at Wembley stadium.

It is impossible to explain what it was like to play there. It was a very nice feeling to be on that pitch. When you walked around before the game in your suit and tie that was when it hit you that it was such a special place. For me, the supporters played a very important part in making Wembley so special. They made the atmosphere. Once you came out of the tunnel, you saw the flags and you heard the incredible noise. Wembley lived up to all my expectations.

By that point I loved England. It was a very difficult time for me when we arrived in 1978, though. We had to learn the language and get used to the culture in a new country. And, of course, later there was the conflict with Argentina. It was a good thing coming with Ossie though, because it helped to make us stronger and we got ourselves through the difficult situations together.

It was a brave decision for us to go to England because it was a very professional league and Tottenham Hotspur was a very big club. Normally Argentinian players go to Italy or Spain, where there are more similarities to our homeland, but we decided on England. And the weather was the worst! If you live in Beunos Aries then it is hot for ten months of the year. In England it is the other way around. But I had a wonderful five years in England.

OSSIE: I had an easier spell than Ricky – I played better than Ricky and he had a difficult time. He found it very difficult to adjust to English football, but that goal in the 1981 Cup final replay changed everything. It was the best goal he'd ever scored.

Everything clicked into place. Up until then he found it very hard at Tottenham, after that it was easy. It gave him the confidence. I settled in quite quickly. I signed for Tottenham at the same time as Ricky and a couple of months later I won a Player of the Month award. In the second season I was fighting to be the best player in England and win the Player of the Year award – I think I lost to Kenny Dalglish. But Ricky never got that far... until the Cup final. He didn't really produce what he was capable of, until that famous game.

People always compared Ricky to me and me to Ricky which was unfair. We were very different players. There was a big hullabaloo about the first game because it was mine and Ricky's first FA Cup final. And of course we were the team of the moment in England at that time because we had so many good players and we played such stylish football. At home it was a big deal too – the FA Cup final was televised live in Argentina because we were playing in it. So there was a lot of pressure on us.

I had always wanted to play at Wembley because it was such a famous stadium. One way or another I couldn't play there with the national team, so I'm glad managed to do it with Spurs in the FA Cup.

The main reason that we were the team of the moment was because we were different to everyone else in the League. We played stylish football. We had Ricky and Glenn [Hoddle] and we played in a very South American way, which a lot of English teams weren't used to. They played more direct football and they played the long ball into the box. We really played very differently to the rest of the country. I loved it. It was a wonderful type of football to play.

Playing with Glenn was wonderful as well. He was such a creative player and a brilliant passer of the ball. We were on the same wavelength and the style of football we were playing was revolutionary. Now you see every team in England playing the way we used to – Arsenal, Chelsea, Liverpool, everybody. But at the time it was very unusual. We tried to play with quick passes and skill. Everybody liked to watch us play – not just supporters of

Tottenham, but supporters of other clubs too and it was very pleasing on the eye. We had fans all over the place.

RICKY: We had a very good team that year. Stevie Perryman was a great player and a brilliant captain. He was so professional. I say to him when I see him now, "I always think what a great captain you were and how you led us to that Cup final." I remember everybody in that team was a good player – Paul Miller, Chris Hughton, Garth Crooks, Stevie Archibald, Ossie, Tony Galvin... they were a very tight unit. Everybody played for each other.

Glenn Hoddle was a wonderful player too. For me he was the best; such a great player. He could pass the ball so well and he was so clever in the way he saw the game. He never did as well for England as he did for Spurs and whenever I watched him play for England I always expected him to do the things he did for us, but he rarely did. I suppose it was very difficult to move into international football and repeat your club form, but I think he was one of the best players in England.

Keith Burkinshaw was a great manager. He was a very English coach – he was very strict and organised. He got us to work very hard and was very tough in training. I say to him now, "How did you expect me to run fast during the game when you made me run every day of the week?" He never gave me a rest. In Argentina, players like me don't have to run in training because I'm in good condition. But in England we had to run every day. I never did that before. I trained very hard before, but not like we did in England. You have to give 100% all the time in training.

But it wasn't just the team that was great at Tottenham, the Spurs fans were also wonderful to me and Ossie. Even now, if I come to the ground and they take me onto the pitch, they clap and they cheer. And White Hart Lane is such a special place with so much history. I'm so happy that the fans remember me for that goal.

So, once we got to Wembley for the first game, we didn't play well. City dominated the midfield and we couldn't get the service to our two strikers – Crooks and Archibald. City worked very hard and they were a very good team in those days. They defended very well and made it very hard for us. It was not a nice game to watch and it wasn't a nice game to play in either. I don't play a physical type of football, so it was not a nice game for me.

City then scored through Tommy Hutchinson; a header after half an hour. We couldn't get going and the manager substituted me and brought on winger Gary Brooke. I felt very sad because I thought that it was the end of the Cup final for me – I didn't think I'd ever get onto the Wembley pitch again because we were losing 0-1 and I thought we had lost our chance. As I walked around the pitch to the dressing room, I felt very sad. In my head I was thinking, "I've played badly and we've lost the Final."

OSSIE: It was sad. The worst thing about the 1981 FA Cup final was Ricky's substitution. It was a very tragic story because it had been his first FA Cup final and a lot had been made of us playing in it and he'd been substituted. He was incredibly disappointed. He was very upset when he left the pitch, he had been crap in the game and did not play well at all. Nothing at all was happening for him, and the manager decided to take him off.

RICKY: Later in the game we won a free-kick through Ossie. I think there was about ten minutes to go. Luckily, Glenn Hoddle took the dead ball and it deflected off Tommy Hutchison past the goalkeeper, Corrigan. I think it was the first time a player had scored for both teams in a FA Cup final. It was a lucky goal, a very lucky goal. And, after 30 minutes of extra time, the FA Cup was having its first ever replay. We were fortunate. Not everybody gets to have a second chance, and when I went off I really thought that was it. Thankfully, we got to play again.

But then, every final is difficult to predict. Everybody plays differently to their form in the League, so it was difficult to analyse that result.

The important thing was that we did not lose and we had a chance to win in the replay. And of course, not every Cup final can be a great game, not everybody can play well in the final. It is a game nobody wants to lose – that is the priority.

OSSIE: I played OK in the first game, but not great. We collapsed in the first match, but me and Glenn kept the game alive. In fact, I would say that we did not deserve to win the game and that Manchester City were the better team. Luckily we managed to claw our way back and get a draw with the own goal which took us to the replay. They were a tough team, they played hard football, so they made it very difficult. We couldn't play our normal fluid football.

We weren't disappointed really. We were more relieved not to have lost the game. We quite easily could have lost, but we were lucky.

Before the second game the manger told us he wanted us to play our usual game in the replay and not worry about the first game. He knew we could play good football. We knew we could play good football and that was the way we were going to be able to beat City. We had to believe in our ability, believe in ourselves and play our usual stylish game. That was how we were going to beat them. We knew we'd be OK.

RICKY: I was very pleased to be playing in the second game – the replay – after being substituted in the first. Some of the papers were saying that maybe Ricky Villa won't be playing in the replay, or that somebody else should be playing. But luckily I was picked.

When I came to play, I wasn't nervous. I wasn't nervous for the first game either, even though it was my first ever FA Cup final. I am a quiet person... OK, maybe I was a little bit nervous before the game, a little bit anxious, but I'd played a lot of very important games for a number of teams with lots of people watching, so I was used to it. You have to be happy to be playing in those sort of games, because it means you are very lucky.

Looking back I had been a little bit unlucky that season because I had torn my ligaments and I'd had an ankle injury. I made my come back for Tottenham in the FA Cup semi-final against Wolves at Highbury. I came back into the team then, but I didn't play many games that season. I remember I had a good game and scored a good goal at Highbury that day. I played a few more games before the Cup final, but I was not 100% fit.

In a strange kind of way, because I had played so badly in the first game the pressure was off for me. I said to myself afterwards, "You've never, ever played that badly before, so it's not very likely that you'll play that badly again." I felt relaxed for the second game.

When I went out onto the pitch for the second game, I knew I had been given a chance to play better, to show the fans what I could do. I had spoken to the manager. He told me that I had to believe in my ability and forget about the first game. He wanted to me to concentrate on the replay and told me not to worry about the fact that I had been substituted in the first game. We had the Sunday off, we went to the club on the Monday to train and we had a meeting with the manager and he told us we had to improve. He wanted the team to work together more.

That was the way we were going to break down Manchester City. He wanted the individual players to perform to the top of their game and I really wanted to prove myself in that game. I said, "Give me the ball and I will do it for you." I really believed in that. I was pleased because I was getting to play at Wembley twice in one week. I was confident too. I was always confident before playing football games. I was in good condition, I was fit, I was clever, I was skilful... come on, I can do it!

OSSIE: Everybody was talking about Ricky and the fact he had been substituted during the first match at Wembley. But we knew he was a good player and he would come good. But the papers wanted to have their say. Every day it was Ricky this, Ricky that. Ricky, Ricky. Ricky.

RICKY: When it finally got to the replay we had no more second chances, we knew this was it. And we played well straightaway. I scored after eight minutes with our first goal, a very easy goal. I can't remember much about it... I can see the goalkeeper, Corrigan making a save and then the ball rebounding off him. I ran onto it, the goal was empty and I put the ball away. When I saw the replay on the TV afterwards I remember Ossie having a shot at goal. The ball hit Steve Archibald who then had a shot and the keeper pushed the ball away into my path and then I scored.

It was a lucky goal. An easy goal. As the ball came to me, the goal seemed bigger than it ever had been before.

OSSIE: It was one of those goals that was an easy goal to score, but at the same time it was one of those goals that can be easy to miss too, because you can think too hard about them. Luckily, he managed to keep the ball down. And, of course, there was a bit of luck involved along the way. But to win any cup competition you have to get a little bit of luck. I was in the penalty area behind Ricky and remember being so pleased for him when it went in.

RICKY: This gave me a confidence boost. It took away all the disappointment from the first game. It meant a lot to me because what I was feeling was that I really had to play well and that was a good start for me. I didn't want to come off in the first game and when I talk about the games now, me and Keith [Burkinshaw] always laugh about that. We never agreed about it before, but now we joke about it. He was a great person and a great manager... but after the substitution I didn't recognise that! I'll never agree with the manager on that one.

Then, suddenly, we were two-one down. Steve MacKenzie scored a great volley for Manchester City. Then the City player Dave Bennett ran onto a long ball and was tackled by our defenders Chris Hughton and Paul Miller. The referee pointed to the spot and gave a penalty which Kevin Reeves put away. But we started to play well and after a corner, Garth Crooks managed to get us an equaliser.

Then there was my goal – the winning goal. I suppose you could say it was a very Argentinian goal, one that was scored in the Argentinian way.

I don't believe English players try to score goals like that – they always want to shoot or put in a cross or pass. I always wanted to do special things when I played football: to dribble, to run at defenders, to make things happen. I enjoyed myself on the pitch when I played like that.

It's funny, when you're running at players like that, you're not thinking about how to finish. You're thinking about going past people. I remember starting my run and going past one player, past two players, past three players and then suddenly the goal was very close and I put the ball in the back of the net. I say, "Easy!"

OSSIE: Oh, it was an amazing goal. I can see it now. He kept going and going and going... and then it was past the keeper. People remember that goal more than any other in the FA Cup. It was amazing.

RICKY: It was something I did in training quite a lot, but to do it in a Cup final was very special. I really liked to play Ricky Villa football – I liked to play individual football. I liked to try to break down defenders with my dribbling. I know the English way is to get the ball down the wings and put crosses in, but dribbling is an important part of the game. If you cross the ball there can be too many people in the box. In that one moment I beat some players and took them out of the game and scored a goal. It is like Ronaldhino, he can beat lots of players, like Rooney. They are top quality players who can score goals from nothing.

When it went in, I didn't think it would be the winner. I thought there might be some more goals because it had been such an open game – extremely different to the first match, but I knew we had a great chance of winning. There was suddenly a lot more pressure on City. They had to find a goal, which meant they had to attack more and the game became more open for us.

I have seen that goal so many times now, mainly because my son is always bringing his friends home and saying, "Oh my dad, he scored a great goal for Tottenham Hotspur in the FA Cup final years ago." And then he shows them on the video. But I don't need to watch it, because I remember it so well. I know how I felt and what happened. It is a moment I am very proud of.

Everybody, everywhere I go, I get stopped and asked about it. I love it. I'm really pleased that it made so many people happy. I enjoy the attention. The English people never forget it.

OSSIE: But if you look at both games you'll see that Glenn played very, very well in both games. If you analyse them, Glenn was wonderful. But, of course, Ricky got all the accolades because of the goals. But he deserved them. I was very, very pleased for him. He suffered quite a lot after the first match and he deserved the praise.

RICKY: When the final whistle went I was delighted. We had won at Wembley! It was a great, great feeling. During the first game I had thought we were going to lose the Cup and then, all of a sudden, we were the winners. Suddenly everything from the first game was forgotten. Because after the first game I was very unhappy. But the second game was much, much different.

OSSIE: The atmosphere was fantastic. It was great for the first game also, but once we'd won the Cup it was incredible. The noise was something I'd never forget. The atmosphere at Wembley was incredibly exciting.

RICKY: Walking up those Wembley stairs was such a moment! It's totally impossible to explain. I try to tell my daughters and my friends what it was like, but it is impossible to explain.

To go to Wembley and to win the Cup was a very special part of my life. Everybody around you is happy. Those moments are so rare in football, so when they happen you have to appreciate them. There was a big party afterwards with family and friends, which was wonderful, and a lot of people in Argentina had been watching the game too – when their players go abroad, the fans always like to know how they're doing.

OSSIE: The celebrations were such good fun, really really wonderful. We really, really let our hair down that night. It was the best celebration I've ever had in my life. Everybody was elated. There was a real family atmosphere and to walk around the pitch with the FA Cup was amazing. To lose and to watch the other team walk around with the trophy must be awful. But for us it was wonderful.

I've had a fantastic career as a player and a manager, but without a shadow of a doubt that's the number one moment of my career.

RICKY: I was very sad to leave Tottenham a couple of years later, but the manager and me came to a decision in the aftermath of the Falklands conflict. It was very professional. I would have liked to maybe stay for one or two more years. But even so, I felt proud. I'd played in the FA Cup final for Tottenham and I scored the winning goal. It felt very important. It was the highlight of my Spurs career.

GRAHAM ROBERTS
CENTRAL DEFENCE/MIDFIELD 1980–1986

BORN   3 July 1959, Southampton
SIGNED   May 1980 from Weymouth; £35,000
SPURS CAREER   287 appearances, 35 goals
HONOURS   FA Cup Winner 1981 & 1982; UEFA Cup Winner 1984;
6 England caps
LEFT   Transferred to Glasgow Rangers, December 1986; £450,000

This former shipyard fitter's mate was signed from non-league Weymouth for just £35,000 and it turned out to be one of Keith Burkinshaw's smarter pieces of business. Converted from a midfielder, Roberts soon built a reputation as a hard-as-nails defender. But he was also a cultured footballer and chipped in with his fair share of goals, particularly in the 1981/82 season, when, because of injuries and politics, he was again called upon to fire the Spurs engine room.

Tottenham Hotspur 1 v Barcelona 1

European Cup-Winners Cup semi-final first leg
Wednesday 7 April 1982

White Hart Lane
Attendance: 41,515

*Spurs challenge for honours on four fronts and push a genuine European
giant all the way thanks to the goalscoring exploits of a centre-back-
turned-midfielder*

Teams

Keith Burkinshaw	**Managers**	Udo Lattek
Ray Clemence	1	Javier Urruti
Chris Hughton	2	Jose Ramos
Paul Miller	3	Antonio Olmo
(Sub. Chris Jones)		
Paul Price	4	Jose Ramon Alexanco
Micky Hazard	5	Manolo
Steve Perryman	6	Jose Sanchez
Graham Roberts	7	Miranda Gerardo
Ricky Villa	8	Juan Estella
Tony Galvin	9	Allan Simonsen
Glenn Hoddle	10	Jose Carrasco
Garth Crooks	11	Enrique Moran
		(Sub. Josep Moratalla)
Roberts 85	**Scorers**	Olmo 59
	Sent Off	Estella 57

Referee: E Mulder (The Netherlands)

IT'S VERY DIFFICULT for me to pick my favourite game for Spurs, because in my six seasons at White Hart Lane I was very lucky to be involved in so many big games, so many memorable games. People tend to forget just how successful we were during the early 80s. In my time at the club we won three trophies, reached three other finals, three semi-finals, finished third in Division One twice, fourth twice, and might have even won the title at some point. That's some achievement, if you consider that people have been saying the current Spurs side is 'on the up' after just missing out qualifying for the Champions League in 2005/06. Obviously, things have changed a lot since my day, but we were always challenging for honours.

Although one game doesn't really stand out, the 1981/82 season, my second at the club, is probably the most memorable, both in terms of the team challenging for trophies and on a personal level.

We ended up winning the FA Cup, becoming the first team to retain the trophy since Bill Nicholson's great Spurs side 20 years earlier, but we could so easily have won the League Cup and the European Cup Winners Cup as well. I also think if it hadn't been for our success in the cup competitions, we would have gone much closer in the league. It's an old cliché, but we were victims of our own success — and it wouldn't be the last time.

When you're chasing silverware on four fronts, by February the big games start coming thick and fast, so you could take your pick from about half a dozen memorable games that season. But for me, not all the memories are good ones. I was left out of the side for a period in March and had to watch from the sidelines as we beat Chelsea in the FA Cup quarter-finals and lost to Liverpool in the League Cup Final. I then came off the bench when we overcame Eintracht Frankfurt to reach the Cup Winners Cup semi-finals. That game proved to be a turning point for me.

If I had to choose one game from that season, it would probably be the first leg of that Cup Winners Cup semi-final, which pitted us against Barcelona. But even that game holds mixed memories for me. For a start, we lost over the two legs, and secondly the game is remembered more for

Barcelona's cynical tactics rather than the quality of the football. But it was still a great occasion. European nights at the Lane always were, and this was the first time the club had qualified for Europe in eight years. Barcelona were also the first really glamorous opposition we'd drawn that year, and the experience of playing against one of Europe's great names would stand us in good stead two years later when we went one stage further in Europe and won the UEFA Cup.

I scored in the second leg of that 1984 final, just as I scored against Barcelona in the game in question. In fact, despite the fact that most people remember me as an uncompromising defender, a lot of my more memorable moments came in the attacking third of the field. Never more was that the case than during the 1981/82 season, when I played quite a few games in midfield.

I actually started off as a midfielder. I played for my hometown club of Southampton as a kid, but I was released as a teenager, when the manager at the time Lawrie McMenemy basically said he didn't think I would make it as a footballer. That was a big set-back, and there would be few more before I broke into the professional ranks.

After leaving Southampton, I went to Bournemouth and was doing very well, before they decided to scrap their youth team and I had to look for another club. From there I went along the South Coast to Portsmouth, where I served my apprenticeship. I was doing really well and Pompey were about to offer me a professional contract when I broke my ankle quite badly and they had to release me.

But one thing you would always say about me was that I was extremely determined. I recovered from injury and joined Dorchester Town, before moving on to Weymouth, who were in the Alliance Premier League, which is now the Conference, so I was playing a pretty good standard. West Brom had come to see me play and I was all set to sign for them – I'd even been up there, met manager Ron Atkinson and been shown around the Hawthorns – when Tottenham came in for me.

It was only by chance that Spurs had even seen me play. Bill Nicholson, who was still scouting for the club, had been on his way to Swindon on a scouting mission when the game was cancelled. He was standing on the train platform, waiting to return to London, when he asked someone where else he could catch a game. Whoever it was told him there was this young midfielder down at Weymouth who should be playing professionally and we happened to have a match that day. Bill came down, watched me play, recommended me to Keith Burkinshaw, and a week later I was at Tottenham. One look at the place and I knew this was where I wanted to play my football.

Keith must have seen something in pre-season training that persuaded him that I would make a good centre-half. I made my debut as a sub against Stoke in October, 1980. We were well off the pace in the league by that stage and leaking a few goals, so, after three straight defeats in the period before Christmas, I was drafted in alongside Paul Miller to shore up the defence. It was the start of a very successful partnership I had with 'Maxi'.

I only joined the club in May 1980 and by May 1981 I had an FA Cup winner's medal. I thought, "this professional football lark is a piece of cake!" Well, not quite, but a year earlier I'd been playing non-league football and the only time I'd ever been to Wembley was as a ball boy while I was at Portsmouth, so to walk out in front of 100,000 people when I was only 21 was almost unbelievable. What an amazing experience for a young lad.

I have lots of memories from that game. I had my two front teeth kicked out by Chrissie Hughton, my own team-mate. It was an accident, of course, but it left me with a gappy grin. I was in the dressing room at half time being examined by the doctor. He turned to Keith and said, "I think he's concussed, he needs to come off." While they were talking, I just got up and walked back down the tunnel and by the time they found me, the second half had kicked off. I wasn't about to give up that kind of experience in a hurry!

Then, on the way back to the hotel, the coach driver had to do an emergency stop, which triggered off a bit of cramp in my hamstring. It was bloody painful, but everyone just cracked up. We were quite flat having been pegged back by Man City, and that lightened the mood. Thankfully, we won the second leg thanks to an unforgettable goal from Ricky Villa.

The club had been struggling a bit when Keith took over after struggling to come to terms with the end of the legendary Bill Nicholson's reign, but with Glenn Hoddle, Chrissie Hughton and Maxi all coming through the youth ranks and Stevie Perryman already established as a great captain, he began to build a good side. Ossie and Ricky joined after the 1978 World Cup, as everyone knows and, when Steve Archibald and Garth Crooks joined around the same time as me, we finally had a couple of strikers who really knew where the goal was. The final piece of the jigsaw arrived in the summer of 1981, when our great goalkeeper, Ray Clemence, joined from Liverpool. We now had a good all-round side that we felt was capable of challenging for all the major honours in what was Spurs' centenary year.

Despite trailing behind strong Liverpool and Ipswich sides, we were still in contention in the League by the turn of the year. The cup games really started to build up then, but rather than having an adverse affect on our league form, winning cup games seemed to galvanise us in the league. In fact, we went unbeaten in all competitions from the middle of December right the way through to the middle of March. That run included wins against Arsenal, Leeds and Chelsea in the FA Cup and Nottingham Forest and West Brom in the League Cup. So even though they were top of the league and a great side, we went into the League Cup Final against Liverpool full of confidence.

A week before that final I was on the bench when we beat Chelsea in the FA Cup quarter-final at Stamford Bridge, Glenn curling in a great winner as we came from behind to win 3-2. Injuries to Glenn, Ossie and Ricky meant I'd already played quite a bit in midfield that season and Ricky, who was still struggling with his match fitness, picked up another knock against Chelsea. I came into the team for the league game against Brighton on the Tuesday, played well in a 3-1 win and just assumed I'd keep my place against Liverpool.

The final was on the Sunday and Keith called me into his office on the Saturday to tell me he was leaving me out and bringing Ricky back in. I wasn't the sort of person who would just accept the decision and get on with it and I let Keith know exactly what I thought. It was probably the only time I was ever really unhappy with him. Before the Chelsea game Ricky had been out for six weeks and Wembley was the kind of place that would find you out if you weren't 100 percent fit, with it's big, energy-sapping pitch and possibility of extra-time.

Keith said to me, "Look, we're still in the FA Cup and if we get to the final you will definitely be playing." But I was like, "What if we don't get to final?" I wasn't thinking about the FA Cup, just the disappointment of missing out on the chance to play at Wembley in a cup final.

Paul Price was playing at centre-back that day. I always felt I was a better player than Pricey, but he had come into the side when I'd moved into midfield and done really well. So he deserved to be on the pitch that day – it's just that I thought I did too.

In those days, being left out meant sitting on the bench in your civvies because you were only allowed one substitute and Keith picked winger Gary Brooke. I was willing the boys to win, of course, kicking every ball with them, but I wasn't a very good spectator because I just wanted to be out there with them.

Archie [Steve Archibald] gave us the lead in the 10th minute and we held it until the 87th minute, when Ronnie Whelan equalised. We ran out of legs after that and Liverpool won 3-1 in extra time. That was Spurs' first ever defeat at Wembley and the first time the club had lost in a domestic cup final. Even as the lads came off the pitch, Keith said to me, "We will get to the FA Cup final and you will play", but I thought I could have made a real difference that day. Would we have won if I'd been on the pitch? Who knows? What Ricky did, he did well, but at the end of the day he wasn't fully 100% percent fit. But managers are paid to make those kind of decisions and unfortunately I was on the wrong end of one that day.

Four days later, we took a 2-0 lead to Frankfurt for the second leg of the Cup Winners Cup quarter-final. And just as I was unlucky to miss out on the League Cup Final, it was through somebody else's misfortune that I got back in the team. That's football....

On the morning of the game we were having a game of five-a-side. Ossie scored and Brookey gave him a bear hug. Ossie was only small, of course, and Brookey didn't realise his own strength and broke Ossie's ribs! He was passed fit and started the game, but within 20 minutes we were 2-0 down. Ossie had given the ball away a few times and could barely run, so I was sent on with orders to stop their playmaker getting on the ball. We managed to stem the flow of Frankfurt's attacks and Glenn came up with yet another important goal to put us through 3-2 on aggregate.

With Ossie's injury more serious than was first thought, I kept my place for our next game just three days later. Not only was this my chance to prove my commitment to the cause and that I was worth my place in the team after the disappointment of the League Cup Final, it was also a chance to put one over on Southampton, who had released me as a youngster.

With the number 7 on my back, I again played in midfield and scored a hat-trick in a 3-2 win. It was the only hat-trick of my career and probably the weirdest hat-trick you will ever see. The first was a diving header – a really satisfying goal. The second was a tap in, and the third was a mis-hit effort that completely deceived the goalkeeper, but they all count, don't they? Unless you're a really top striker, you don't score many hat-tricks in your career and this one was even more special because it was against my home-town club. I always got a bit of stick when I went down there to visit my family, and whenever I played at The Dell, my family would come and watch me and my friends who were Southampton supporters would give me loads of stick. But the most pleasing thing was that I proved Lawrie

McMenemy wrong and to be fair to him, he came up to me afterwards and said as much.

As I mentioned earlier, we were victims of our own success in a way. One of Keith's great strength was his loyalty to his players and we would go through a season with a squad of only 13 or 14 core players. Hardly anybody had a big squad in those days and in that season alone we played 66 competitive games. I played in 56 of those and some of the lads played even more. That is just unheard of these days.

But it wasn't the number of games that was the problem as such. As any player will tell you, you'd much rather be playing games than training and I was no different. I loved playing so much that I was never 'rested' – I only ever missed games if I was dropped, suspended or injured. And it was the injuries that really took their toll, because like I said, we only had a really small squad.

The Southampton game was our fourth straight league win, but our exploits in the cup competitions meant the league games really started to pile up around this time. We were playing two, sometimes three, games a week and this particularly affected us going forward. Archie and Crooksy, who were so prolific in their first season, both had long spells out through injury and although Mark Falco came in and did well, we didn't really have anybody else. Despite the fact that, in retrospect, we had a reputation for being a good to watch, but a bit shaky at the back, we actually conceded 20 fewer goals than the previous season, when we finished 10th in the league. In 1982, we finished fourth, despite scoring three goals fewer. If we hadn't had those injuries up front, who knows what would have happened?!

After beating Southampton, we didn't win for three games, which effectively put us out of the title race and we fell away a bit after that. At least that meant we could concentrate on the cups, but we were soon faced with another problem...

Before our FA Cup semi-final with Leicester, Ossie had been named in the Argentina squad for their next lot of internationals, with their coach agreeing that he'd let Ossie return for the final if we got there – which we did thanks to a comfortable 2-0 win. Crooksy gave us the lead, then a really weird own goal from Ian Wilson – a lob from outside the area – sealed it. But 24 hours before that game, the Falklands had conflict began and Ossie was booed by the Leicester fans every time he touched the ball.

He still joined up for international duty, but we now knew it was unlikely that he'd return before the end of the season. Ricky wasn't called up, but Keith knew that he would be in for some stick as well, and didn't think it was worth the risk of playing him. We would now have to do without two of our most creative players for the rest of the season.

I sometimes wonder what might have happened if we'd had Ossie and Ricky available for the games against Barcelona. They weren't a great side at that point, but they still had a reputation for playing attractive, attacking football – very much like us – so we expected two open games. But they turned out to be very tight, tense affairs and Ossie and Ricky would have given us that extra bit of creativity that might have made the difference. But that's history I suppose.

The first leg came just four days after the FA Cup semi-final. It was a Wednesday night at White Hart Lane and, as usual for an evening game, the atmosphere was electric. There was nothing like a European night at the Lane in front of a full house.

Barcelona came with just one thing in mind: to stop us playing. To be fair, we were all surprised with their approach. In a way it speaks volumes for what a good side we were and much they must have feared us. They basically kicked us off the park and the Dutch referee let them get away with murder. Kicking, punching, shirt-pulling… they had every trick in the book and, as one newspaper put it, some that weren't. On the telly, Frank McLintock said it was, "the most cynical game I've seen for ten years." Like me, Frank was a hard, no-nonsense defender, but this was something else.

We attacked from the off and they set out to stop us. That was pretty much the pattern of the game the whole way through. By half-time we were getting pretty frustrated, which was exactly what they wanted. The game became niggly and, to be fair, we began to react. But what can you do? The ref wasn't taking any action and you can't let teams bully you.

At the break, Keith just told us to keep our cool, keep playing our football and eventually the goal would come. Ten minutes into the second half, the referee finally got a grip on the game and sent off Estella for an awful tackle on Tony Galvin. It was a high, late lunge, and Tony was lucky not to escape without serious injury.

With an extra man, we really pushed on and knew it would be only a matter of time before we scored. Unfortunately, when the goal did come, it was Barcelona who scored it, completely against the run of play. Olmo, their captain, let fly from about 40 yards, but it was more of a hopeful ball into the box than anything. It was on target and as it floated towards Clem, we expected him to catch it easily, but it somehow squirmed through his hands and dropped over the line. I think Clem was so confident of taking it that it was almost like he was getting ready to throw it out before it even got to him and just took his eye off the ball for a split second. It was a bad error and a lucky break for them, but nobody blamed Clem. He hardly ever made mistakes and to be fair, he had kept us in the game in previous round in Frankfurt.

We now threw everything forward in search of an equaliser and it didn't look like it would come, but then five minutes from the end, we got a got a free-kick out wide. There was a lot of jostling and pushing in the area, but, as Glenn swung the ball in, I managed to shrug off three Barcelona players and drift free at the back post. The ball came straight to me and I slotted it in first time.

I carried on running round the back of the goal to celebrate in front of the fans, but when I turned round, the three Barcelona players who I'd been having argy-bargy with in the penalty area were running after me! Even as I ran back to the halfway line, they were chasing me and arguing with the referee, claiming I'd been pushed them. That was a bit rich coming from them and the ref was having none of it.

Even their manager admitted that the game got out of hand, and both clubs were fined – them more than us, it has to be said. Estella was also suspended for two games for his red card. Strangely, though, they started the second leg the same way they started the first. In front of 120,000 at the Nou Camp you'd expect them to at least have a go, but they didn't. They just sat back and tried to stop us playing. With the away goal, they only need a 0-0 draw and that's exactly what the played for.

It made for a strange atmosphere, despite the huge crowd. It was even more eerie halfway through the first half when there was a floodlight failure. The pitch was in complete darkness for five minutes and when the floodlights came back on, again it was us that made most of the running – we just couldn't find a way through. Like I said, with Ossie and Ricky in the side, we might have had that extra bit of creativity to unlock their defence. As we pushed forward more, searching for the goal that would take us through, they hit us with the sucker punch. Pricey failed to clear the ball properly in our area and the Dane Allan Simonsen, their best player over the two legs, nipped in and poked it past Clem as he came off his line. It was an awful way to go out, and after going so close in all the other the competitions, we were it left with the FA Cup as our only chance of silverware.

Although we were out of the title race, we were still chasing a UEFA Cup place and fourth spot in the league was still very much up for grabs, so we couldn't afford to just concentrate on the Cup Final and hope to qualify for Europe that way. Inevitably your mind wanders a bit, but you need to keep yourself ticking over and keep that winning habit. The problem was, we played Liverpool and Ipswich away in the space of three days in our last two league games. They were first and second in the league and we lost both games, which made it three straight defeats – not exactly ideal preparation for an FA Cup Final.

Despite disappointment in the other competitions, we were still strong favourites going into the final against Queen's Park Rangers. They were a Second Division team at the time, and we had the experience of winning it the year before. We also wanted to win it for Ossie and Ricky. They were two great players and two great lads, who were caught in the middle of an unfortunate situation.

But sometimes, the games you are expected to win easily are the most difficult and, after playing so many games in such a short period of time, we looked a bit tired in the first game. In fact, we were lucky to escape with a draw. The first 90 minutes were a bit of a non-event and, as in the League Cup Final, we were out on our feet. But Keith didn't let us slump to the ground as the lads had done against Liverpool and the fans really started to get behind us. We took the lead in the first half of extra time. Again, I was involved in the attacking third, slipping a ball inside to Glenn whose shot deflected in off Tony Currie. But credit to QPR, they threw everything at us and got a deserved equaliser when Terry Fenwick got his head to Bob Hazell's flick-on from a long throw.

Our preparation for the replay was much better. Keith made sure we got plenty of rest and plenty of massages, nothing too strenuous. It worked a treat and we came out firing and scored pretty early. I picked up the ball and moved forward into their half, going past a couple of players and jumping over Hazell's lunging tackle.

As I moved into the penalty area Tony Currie slid in and, as I nudged the ball past him, he brought me down. It was a stonewall penalty and, to be fair to the QPR players, none of them appealed. People would have expected Tony Currie to making last-ditch tackles about as much as they would have expected me to beat three players and win a penalty, but as I've already mentioned, I actually had quite a bit of success going forward during my career, particularly that season. Glenn sent keeper Peter Hucker the wrong way from the penalty and we thought we would win the game comfortably after that.

QPR barely threatened in the first half, but they came out and really gave it a go in the second half and put us on the back foot. We barely created a chance and were hanging on at times. There were last ditch tackles, great saves, and I ended up dropping back alongside the centre-halves. If their main goal threat, Clive Allen, had been fit, it might have been a different story. But he had to go off injured after just two minutes of the first game and didn't recover in time for the replay, so they didn't have anybody who could put the ball in the net.

Still, having played well for 90 percent of the season, victory was no more than we'd deserved. After challenging on four fronts, to finish the season empty-handed would have been an injustice. I wouldn't say it felt better or worse than the previous year, just different. The 1981 final was my first visit to Wembley as a player and you can't replicate that feeling of winning your first FA Cup. There was a great sense of relief in 1982 and because I was a bit older and more experienced, I was probably able to soak it up a bit more. It was also very satisfying to be one of the few teams in history to retain the Cup.

Although we were very successful, I look back now and think we could, and perhaps should, have won two or three more trophies. We picked up one other piece of silverware during my time at Spurs, the UEFA Cup in 1984. That was another great occasion for me. Captain Steve Perryman was suspended for the second leg of the final, so I skippered the side and I'd like to think I led from the front. I scored the equaliser late on that took the game into extra time and then took the first penalty in the shoot-out, sending the keeper the wrong way. And there I was at the end, lifting the trophy in front of our own fans, What a moment. That's something that will stick in the memory for a very long time.

The following season, we again went close to winning the UEFA Cup, this time losing to Real Madrid in the quarter-final in another tight contest, 0-1 over the two legs. Madrid weren't cynical like Barcelona, but they were just as content to sit back and hit us on the break. And again, we were very unlucky. Steve Perryman scored a bizarre own goal in the first leg at home and was then harshly sent off in the Bernabeu. Mark Falco then had a perfectly good equaliser ruled out for offside by the referee, even though the linesman hadn't even flagged and none of their players had appealed. If that had stood, who knows what would have happened.

But perhaps my biggest disappointment was the fact we never won the league. We were certainly good enough, probably one of the best teams never to win the league. In 1985, we finished third, behind second placed Liverpool on goal difference and 13 points behind champions Everton, but that doesn't tell the whole story. We were only three points behind them when they came to White Hart Lane in April. We absolutely battered them in the first half, but somehow went in 2-0 down. I managed to pull one back with a 35-yarder – one of my best ever goals – but they hung on and went from strength to strength whereas we fell away a bit.

I left halfway through the 1986/87 season, Spurs again finished third and again we were undone by extended cup runs. We reached the semi-finals of the League Cup, losing after a replay with Arsenal, and, of course, lost to Coventry in a famous FA Cup Final.

As I've said, we were much better defensively than people gave us credit for, but perhaps our attacking approach did cost us at times. It was more down to our philosophy than an inability to defend. We perhaps couldn't close games out as well as we should have and lost the odd game we should have scraped a draw from.

Having come from non-league, though, and having suffered quite a few set-backs early in my career, I think I appreciated the good times that bit more. We won trophies, got to finals, challenged in the league and played with style. I went to a reunion for the 1981 FA Cup-winning team recently and I was there until two o' clock in the morning talking to fans. Those who remember that far back all said how they wished Spurs had that team now, because success has been so thin on the ground recently – just one trophy in 15 seasons. That period in my career will always be special to me and I'm very proud to have played my part.

TONY PARKS
GOALKEEPER 1981-1988

BORN   28 January 1963, Hackney
SIGNED   September 1980 from Apprentice
SPURS CAREER   49 games
HONOURS   UEFA Cup Winner 1984
LEFT   Transferred to Brentford, 1988

Tony Parks will forever be remembered as the rookie goalkeeper who won the 1984 UEFA Cup for Spurs with his penalty shootout heroics at White Hart Lane. But whilst many assume Parks was deputising for the injured Ray Clemence, the 21 year-old had actually forced himself into Keith Burkinshaw's first team ahead of the former Liverpool and England legend on merit to write himself into Spurs folklore.

Tottenham Hotspur 1 v Anderlecht 1

UEFA Cup Final second leg
Wednesday 23 May 1984

White Hart Lane
Attendance 46,258

*Rookie goalkeeper replaces a legend and wins the UEFA Cup for Spurs
in the most dramatic fashion possible*

Teams

Keith Burkinshaw	**Managers**	Paul van Himst
Tony Parks	1	Jacky Munaron
Danny Thomas	2	Georges Grün
Graham Roberts	3	Morton Olsen
Paul Miller	4	Walter De Greet
(Sub. Ossie Ardiles)		
Chris Hughton	5	Wim Hofkens
Gary Mabbutt	6	Rene Van der Eycken
(Sub. Ally Dick)		
Micky Hazard	7	Enzo Scifo
Tony Galvin	8	Frank Arnesen
		(Sub. Arnor Gudjohnsen)
Gary Stevens	9	Michel De Groote
Steve Archibald	10	Alex Czerniatynski
		(Sub. Kenneth Brylle-Larsen)
Mark Falco	11	Frankie Vercauteren
Roberts 84	**Scorers**	Czerniatynski 60

Referee: V Roth (West Germany)

I WAS BORN IN Hackney, which is about the same distance from White Hart Lane and Highbury, but like all my family I supported Arsenal as a kid. My dad grew up a Gunner and when my brother and me were old enough as kids, he'd take us with him to Highbury and we'd stand in the Clock End.

The one thing that sticks in my memory is the 1971 FA Cup Final against Liverpool, when Charlie George scored the winner to clinch the Double. My dad travelled the length and breadth of the country watching the Gunners that season and every week he would come back with a match programme. From that point on, I knew Arsenal were the team for me.

As a young kid I played my football on Hackney Marshes, and, when I was 11, I was spotted by Queen's Park Rangers, who asked me to train with them for a year. But I really disliked it at QPR, so much so that about 10 months in I seriously wondered whether professional football was for me.

I left and decided to just keep on enjoying my weekend football and luckily enough, quite soon after, I was invited to go for a trial at Tottenham. I was a little apprehensive at first because of my Arsenal background, but some of the boys I played with on the Marshes who were at Spurs spoke very highly of them and from the moment I walked through the door, I realised QPR and Spurs were like chalk and cheese. I fell in love with the club almost immediately and by the time I was 13 I was sold on the idea of Tottenham. It was a great learning environment, they taught football the right way and I never thought about going anywhere else.

When I first arrived at Spurs, they were actually on a bit of downward spiral. In 1977 they were relegated from the First Division for the first time since the war and moving in the wrong direction. Tottenham had always been recognised as one of the country's great footballing sides, right from the days of Arthur Rowe's 'push and run' team of the early 1950s, and after Bill Nicholson's departure I think they lost their way a bit trying to emulate past glories.

But Keith Burkinshaw dragged the club up by its shirt-tails. Like Bill Nick, Keith was a Yorkshireman and I don't think he liked the London 'scene'. A lot of people thought London footballers were a bit too flash and didn't have the love for the game that perhaps they should, but Keith brought that professional drive back to the club and was able to couple that with the club's philosophy of playing attacking football.

Keith built his team around round talented youngsters like Glenn Hoddle and good pros like Steve Perryman. He took Spurs back up in 1978 and at that point the board decided they were going to rejuvenate the ground, building the new West Stand.

Things started to look up and, in Glenn, the fans suddenly had a new hero to worship. With the addition of Ricky and Ossie, Garth Crooks and Steve Archibald, Keith really signalled his intentions about how he wanted to play and that really took hold between 1980 and '85. We never really threatened to win the league championship in that period, but we were always mentioned as possible winners in the all the cup competitions – at home and in Europe.

The transition from apprentice to young professional is pretty rocky, because you're not sure if you're going to get offered a contract and you face a nervous wait to find out. But Keith was always very good to me. If the first team were playing at home, the manager would always come and watch the youth team at Cheshunt in the morning. And if you played well he would always tell you, always be very encouraging. One day while I was playing he spoke to my dad on the sidelines and told him that I'd be getting a professional contract.

I was only 17 at the time, but when Ray Clemence was signed from Liverpool year later, Keith made me his number 2 ahead of more experience goalkeepers like Milija Aleksic, Barry Daines and Mark Kendall. I made my league debut at just 17 against West Ham and I also played in the second leg of a European Cup Winners Cup game after we'd won the first leg easily. So he gave me good experience early on. He let all three of the other keepers go and told Ray he thought I had a chance of making it and to help me all he could.

That faith wasn't always repaid in kind by me, but he always gave me the opportunity to prove myself, and that's always a real boost to your confidence when you're a young professional trying to make your way in the game.

I was a little overawed to begin with. I mean, this was Ray Clemence, an experienced England international who had done it all at club level and I was just a young lad trying to prove my worth. He was always supportive and always encouraging, but I was a young London lad and a bit of a tear-away at that. And like with Keith, perhaps if I'd listened a bit more a done one or two things a bit differently, I would have been a better goalkeeper. Hindsight's a wonderful thing.

It's funny, because for the last four years I've been working under Clem as full-time goalkeeping coach for the FA and when the job first came up I think he was a bit reluctant to take me on at first. It was his head on the block and images of me doing one or two silly things in the past were probably foremost in his mind. It was my opportunity to show him I'd grown up, learnt from those experiences, and could handle the responsibility.

In truth, I think I knew that, as long as Ray was at the club, I'd always be number two. It was nice to play some first team games when I got the chance, but I think that's the difference between the really top players and the rest. They have a different mentality, they always want to be the best, and I think Clem had that in abundance. He knew that he was a special goalie and that I was unlikely to replace him, barring injury. In fact, the only time I was ever able to replace him on merit was during the 1983/84 season, when we won the UEFA Cup.

Even now, people must think I only came on as a sub for Clem in the penalty shootout because I was good at saving penalties or something! That can be a bit frustrating because I'd already played a quite a few games that season and kept Ray out of the team for a while. Having been number two to a truly gifted keeper for so long, to get the opportunity to play in front of him was very special.

I played three first team games before the start of the 1983/84 season, but I began the campaign as number 2 to Clem as per normal. After going nine games unbeaten in the league in the autumn, we had a miserable December and New Year, losing five out of seven, drawing the other two and conceding a lot of goals. To be fair to Clem, he wasn't having the best of times with his own form and I was playing well for the reserves. Being full of yourself like you are at that age, I thought that, injury or no injury, I had a good chance of overtaking him. But when a manager is under pressure and trying to make his living, he's always going to find it difficult to risk a young unknown when he has experienced pros in his squad and I remained on the sidelines.

Then, in the third round of the FA Cup at Fulham, Clem suffered a shoulder injury just before half-time and Graham Roberts had to go in goal for the second half. We managed to hold on for a 1-1 draw to take them back to White Hart Lane for a replay on the Wednesday. The injury would keep Clem out for a while, so that was me in the team. It was an unfortunate way for me to be given my opportunity, but you have to make the most of your opportunities.

I didn't know how long I'd be in the side, but I thoroughly enjoyed the game, kept a clean sheet (we won 2-0) and got a good reaction from everyone: the other players, the crowd and the press. I kept another clean sheet the following week against Ipswich at home and another against Norwich in the fourth round of the Cup to make it three in four games.

It now emerged that Clem's injury was a little worse than first feared. At this point Keith could have brought in somebody else, somebody more experienced, but instead I got an extended run in the team, which was a great confidence booster. I was still in the team by early March when the quarter-finals of the UEFA Cup came around. We'd beaten Bayern Munich in the previous round before Christmas and then there was a long break before our next game against Austria Vienna.

Clem was back in training the week of the first leg and the day before the game he went to see the manager and declared himself fit for selection. I assumed that he would go straight back into the team. I was just happy that I'd had a good run in the team, had play reasonably well and got a good reaction from everybody around me. But when the team was announced, there was my name at number one, with Ray on the bench.

Looking back, it must have been very difficult for Keith to have to tell an experienced England international that he wasn't going to be getting his place back automatically because the person in his position had played particularly well and he didn't see the need to change it.

Ray would have been disappointed, but he was the consummate professional. He never showed any ill feeling towards me, and in fact I think he took pleasure from the fact that I was doing very well. He earned a lot of compliments from people telling him what a good job he'd done in helping my development. I was his protégé and he worked hard to give me the encouragement and advice I needed to help me progress.

A big European night at White Hart Lane was a fantastic event. It was always packed out – I remember vividly all the fans crammed into the Shelf Side – and the atmosphere was electric. We always wore all white at home in Europe and it was something special to see someone like Glenn Hoddle get ready. He looked immaculate. We had a good team by this point, with some very good players, the likes of Perryman, Ardiles and Archibald –

and it was now my chance to prove I could stand shoulder to shoulder with them.

This quarter-final tie was a big night for me. Added to the fact that it was my first big European night and the pressure of keeping Ray out of the side, was the pressure that comes from within. The pressure you put on yourself is always the biggest and as a player I was always a bit too much of a worrier. I always got nervous and uptight before a game. That's probably what sets the top players apart – they relish it. Once the whistle went I would always be OK, but the pre-match nerves were something I never really conquered.

But I played well, kept a clean sheet and we won 2-0. Just before half-time I gashed my knee quite badly, but I had it stitched up and was able to play the rest of the game without too much discomfort and didn't think any more of it.

During the game, the Austrians weren't happy with some of the tackling by our two centre-backs, Graham Roberts and Paul Miller. That night I think they were hard, but mostly fair, but it was always interesting playing behind those two. You'd hear them in the dressing room before the game, discussing our opponents and how they were going to wind them up.

I remember a conversation they had about Mark Hughes once. Sparky is a similar age to me, so he was pretty young at the time, but I'd played against him in FA Youth Cup games and knew that he was always a pretty physical lad. Anyway, this one particular match against Manchester United, Paul and Graham came off at half-time saying, "we've kicked him, punched him, called him everything under the sun and he still keeps coming back for more!" They were shocked that their bullying tactics weren't working on him as they often did on other players.

Anything went with those two – all the dirty tricks: pinching, hair pulling, whacks on the back of the calf and so on. They quite liked the idea of being the hard men of Tottenham and played up to it, so it was interesting to see what happened when somebody dared give them some back like Sparky did. It shocked them, and proved that they weren't quite as hard as they made out!

Having played well against Austria Vienna, I was confident that I was in the team on merit and would keep my place for the foreseeable future. But by the following morning, the stitches in my knee had become infected and I was ruled out of the league game against Liverpool at Anfield on the Saturday. Anfield was a place I'd always wanted to play, having seen the fans in the Kop on TV, swaying in their thousands. It was a fantastic arena in which to play football, so that was probably the biggest disappointment of all.

Obviously now that Clem was fit again, he went straight back into the side against his former club, then played against West Brom the following week and again in the second leg at Austria Vienna. Having finally got into the side on merit, that aspect of the injury was disappointing, but more than anything I was just happy to have had a decent run in the side and that people now knew a bit more about what I could do. Hopefully, that would bode well for me getting a new contract at the end of the season.

But after training on the Friday after the second leg, Clem was doing some shot stopping and with the very last shot of the session, he broke his little finger quite badly. All of a sudden I was back in the team.

It was a strange feeling. It's the old cliché about every cloud having a silver lining and that's very much the case in football. As disappointed as I was for Clem, there was also the elation of knowing I was going to get another run in the team. We did really well, winning four of the next five games in the league and from that point onwards I knew that I was pretty much certain to be in the team for the rest of the season, barring me picking up another injury.

The first leg of the UEFA Cup semi-final away to Hajduk Split was a fantastic experience for me. It was the first time I'd seen things like flares in the crowd and I remember one which was thrown landed right on the back of my foot. Having never played in that kind of environment before, it scared the life out of me

We went 1-0 ahead quite early on with a very scrappy goal and held out comfortably until half-time, but a mad 10-minute spell in which they scored twice – one of which took a wicked deflection – turned things around. Like many Eastern European clubs, they were a good side: strong, technically gifted and good passers of the ball. But with an away goal, we fancied our chances going into the return game.

The second leg didn't quite go according to plan. Micky Hazard put us in front with a terrific free-kick in the sixth minute, but because a 1-0 win was all we needed, we were very nervous after that and didn't know quite how to play it.

About ten minutes from time, they had a shot from distance, which moved in the air just before it got to me. As I went to catch it, it came off my hands, hit the crossbar, back down, off my hands again and along the line before I finally fell on it. It was poor goalkeeping and I remember thinking "thank Christ" as the whole crowd breathed a huge sigh of relief. We were through, but quite fortunately so in all honesty.

We could and – as it turned out later after match-fixing revelations – should have been playing Nottingham Forest in the final, but I was glad we were playing Anderlecht. It made it feel like a proper European final and they were the reigning champions. Anderlecht were a top European side at the time, with players like Danish internationals Morton Olsen and Frank Arnesen and Belgian midfielder Enzo Scifo, who was only 17, but already a fantastic player. They were also unbeaten at home in Europe in 10 years, so it was an enormous challenge.

More than 8,000 Spurs fans travelled to Brussels for the game and one fan had even been shot dead the night before the match, so there was a heavy police presence at the stadium with fears of reprisal. The game went off without further incident, but inside Anderlecht's intimate stadium the atmosphere was electric. Our fans, in particularly, were amazing.

I was quite nervous in the dressing room beforehand. I remember being sat there as the kit was being laid out. We were in all light blue and the away kit's goalkeeper's shirt was red. I had an aversion to red shirts, because it stood for Arsenal and I played for Tottenham. The red shirt bugged me and got inside my head, so much so that I made them go out and get me a green shirt. That's how agitated I was.

We were actually the better team in the first leg. In fact, it was was probably our best performance in the competition that year. Keith recognised that our strengths were going forward and we really took the game to Anderlecht. We had a number of chances in the first half and took the lead early in the second when Paul Miller headed in powerfully from a corner. Anderlecht came at us, as you would expect, but we were coping pretty comfortably and always looked dangerous ourselves.

They equalised three minutes from time and I was pretty annoyed to be criticised for that goal. From a corner, the ball was cleared to the edge of the box and fired back in through a crowd of players. I managed to parry it, but they reacted quickest and turned in the rebound. I felt that we could have defended the corner better as a whole and, when it came back in, there was a ruck of players, so I was completed unsighted. I am the first to hold my hands up if I've made a mistake, but I don't think I was at fault on this occasion.

A draw and an away goal was a great result, and, although we probably should have won the game, we went back to White Hart Lane knowing we had a real chance.

As in all the other rounds, there was a two-week gap between the first and second rounds of the UEFA Cup Final, which was strange for us, because we were out of both domestic cups and had nothing to play for in the league. It was just a matter of keeping ourselves ticking over, playing our last league game and avoiding injuries. In that respect, our preparation was perfect. But having lost Garth Crooks and Glenn Hoddle to long-term injuries earlier in the season, and with Ossie Ardiles only fit enough to take his place on the bench, we now had to make do without our captain, Steve Perryman, who had picked up his second booking of the competition in Brussels and would miss the second leg.

In games like this, when you have big players missing, you look around the dressing room and think, "God, I wish we had him playing tonight." I'm sure there were some players in that dressing room wishing Clem was playing that night. I'm sure some of the senior pros at the back thought that having his experience behind them might calm them down a bit.

It was probably the only game I've played in where the nerves never went away. I was nervous throughout the whole day: when I got the ground, during the warm-up, standing in the tunnel. When the referee blows his whistle – that's when the nerves usually disappear, but not on this occasion. I was nervous throughout the whole game. I think the whole magnitude of the occasion just got to me.

And to be fair to Anderlecht, they were absolutely fantastic on the night. Some of their football was brilliant and they were the better team until the hour mark, when they took the lead. They worked the ball down the right-hand side and Morton Olsen fed Czerniatynski, who clipped it beyond me as I went to close him down. It was very well taken and I had no chance. Suddenly, you felt the crowd's mood drop – Anderlecht just looked so good. But for all their lovely football, I actually had less to do than their keeper, particularly once we went behind.

We laid siege to the Anderlecht goal, but we just couldn't find a way past their keeper. We were getting more and more desperate as time ticked away. As a last throw of the dice, Keith threw on Ossie and it seemed to lift us a bit. Seven minutes from time, the ball broke to Steve Archibald, who had scored 28 goals that season and had been in great form, but Munaron pulled off a magnificent save from his piledriver. From the resulting corner, the ball fell to Ossie no more than two yards out, but he seemed to snatch at it and somehow walloped it against the bar. At that point I thought it wasn't gonna be our night. But Anderlecht didn't clear their lines properly and the ball went out to Micky Hazard, who had taken the corner. He drove it in low,

Mark Falco managed to hold off the defender and there was Graham Roberts, who had a good goalscoring record for a defender. He chested it down and fired it through the crowd of players into the bottom corner. The relief was just immense.

It's funny, but as soon as the whistle went for the end of extra time my nerves finally settled. Being a goalkeeper in a penalty shootout is a no-lose situation. Nobody is going to blame you if you don't save one, but I always fancied myself to save at least one out of five in a shootout situation.

We knew there was the possibility of the game going to penalties and although we hadn't practised them as such, I'd saved a couple for the first team already, so I knew I was capable of doing it again. Suddenly, I oozed confidence for the first time that evening.

I suppose it was all set up for me. I remember watching a video of ITV's coverage of the game afterwards and Brian Moore and Jimmy Greaves were doing the commentary. As me and Munaron, the Anderlecht keeper, are walking towards the goal, Jimmy says, "I fancy Anderlecht now. Their goalkeeper has had a really good game and will be feeling really confident whereas the lad in goal for Tottenham is really inexperienced." It just proves what a leveller a penalty shootout can be.

There has been loads of scientific research into what a goalkeeper should do to give himself the best chance of saving a penalty, but if you pick a side, guess right, and commit yourself, you have a good chance. What I would try and do, however, was get onto the goal line early, so I could look at the taker as he was walking up – not to look at his body language or to try and psyche him out, but to see if, at any point, he looked up to see where he was going to put it.

As Morton Olsen picked up the ball he looked straight into my left-hand corner and from that point on, I knew which way I was going to dive. He struck it quite nicely, low and hard into the corner, but I got across and made a really good save. The crowd went bonkers and as I looked up I could see lads back on the halfway line. Now they were thinking, "crikey, we've got a shot at this."

For the next three penalties I faced, for some reason I kept diving the same way as I dived for the first one, because I had so much joy diving there the first time. I wasn't really thinking about what was happening – I was caught in the moment of that first save and their penalty-takers put two in the other side and one the straight down the middle. But because Graham Roberts, Mark Falco, Gary Stevens and Steve Archibald all scored their penalties, one save could still be enough if Danny Thomas scored our fifth spot-kick. You have to say it wasn't a great penalty. He took it well enough, but it was a nice height for a goalkeeper and he guessed right to make a comfortable save. Danny just stood there with his hands on his head. He was devastated. Suddenly, the crowd went quiet, but as Danny walked back to the centre circle, they realised we needed a lift and began to chant his name. "There's only one Danny Thomas!" It echoed all around the ground and was an incredible lift. When the fans back the team like that it can make all the difference and everyone who was there remembers that chant.

The Anderlecht players were delighted, of course, because suddenly, they were back in the hunt. They needed to score their last penalty to take it to sudden death.

As Arnor Gudjohnsen, Eidur's dad, stepped up to take it, I realised I'd gone the same way for all their penalties and decided to go the other way. I presumed he'd been watching and had assumed that I'd just picked a side and was going to stick to it.

He hit such a poor penalty that even my mum could have saved it. As I dived to my right, it was at such a lovely height it was almost like everything was in slow motion. As I rolled over and jumped up, the thing I can remember most is the look on Danny Thomas's face. From being in sheer and utter distress one minute earlier, it was now a complete picture.

"I've done it!" I thought, and all I wanted to do was run. The next thing I know I'm being clothes-lined and elbowed by the rest of the team. In fact, the first one on the scene was Ray Clemence. If the other players hadn't caught up with me I would have run right out of the gate at the other end of the ground and straight down the Tottenham High Road to Seven Sisters tube station. I had the piss taken out of me for ages for that celebration, but in a moment like that you don't know what you're doing.

Down on the touchline, Steve Perryman and Keith Burkinshaw were sharing an embrace. Keith had announced in January that he would be leaving the club at the end of the season and I suppose there was an element of us "doing it for him" as much as ourselves. Steve was Keith's captain but, as I mentioned earlier, was suspended for that game. It was a nice moment.

As we went up to collect the trophy and our medals, I was behind Graham Roberts, our captain for the night because Steve Perryman was suspended. As I collected my medal there was also a small replica of the UEFA Cup, which I assumed was the Man of the Match trophy for me, so I picked it up and took it to the dressing room. I soon realised that it was actually a replica of the actual Cup for the club to keep after the original went back, but I thought it would look quite good on my mantelpiece, so I stuffed it in my kit back and went for a shower.

When I got back, Irvine Scholar, the chairman, was sat there in a wheel-chair, having recently broken his leg during a charity match, with the replica in his lap. He'd come in asking if anybody had seen it and everybody had pointed to my bag. I knew I would have had to take it back eventually, but it was worth a try!

All the players and their families stayed at the club, where they put on a big do for us. At about two o' clock in the morning somebody asked me if I would be willing to go on TV:AM for an interview. I was on such a high that I said "no problem" and was told that they'd send a car to my house at 7am. But I didn't leave to the club until about six and I was obviously a little bit the worse for wear. I quickly went home, got changed and the car picked me up to take me to the studios, but with all the singing and the celebrating I'd completely lost my voice. As I rolled in to the studios, Anne Diamond looked at me most disgustedly, as if to say, "typical bloody footballer". The interview had to be cancelled, but the people there were very nice to me, took me to the canteen, gave me some breakfast, put me back in the car and packed me off home!

It was like hell for a couple of weeks after the game. During that period I had a small insight into what someone like David Beckham goes through. Everywhere I went I was recognised. I got home and there were press camped outside my house. Then I went to the pub with my family and friends the next day and everyone was coming up to me and asking me about the game. I probably became a bit big-headed with all the adulation. I thought I had made it because of that game and never really drew under a line under it and went back to working hard and doing the things that had got me there in the first place.

Peter Shreeves succeeded Keith Burkinshaw as manager that summer. Peter had been at Tottenham in various capacities and was an excellent coach, but we never really saw eye to eye and the things I was up to off the pitch probably made the decision for him to put Clem back in the side. I went out too much, didn't train hard enough and generally just took my eye off the ball.

With hindsight, maybe it was a case of too much too soon. Perhaps I thought it was going to be like that every year. I would love to have had that experience every season, but if it was only to come once I think I would have been able to appreciate more if it had come later in my career. Saying that, some people play 500 games and never get near a European final, let alone making the winning save. It's not a bad thing to be remembered for!

CLIVE ALLEN
STRIKER 1984–1988

BORN   20 May 1961, Stepney, London
SIGNED   16 August 1984 from Queen's Park Rangers; £700,000
SPURS CAREER   141 games 85 goals
HONOURS   5 England caps
LEFT   Transferred to Bordeaux, 10 May 1988; £1,000,000

Very few footballers are remembered for a number, but Clive Allen's 49 goals for Spurs in the 1986-87 season was a unique achievement in an era when players simply no longer found the net that many times in one campaign. Pace, positioning and all-round finishing had always been Allen's trademarks, and for one season he was simply unstoppable. Ultimately, though, his feats went unrewarded as Spurs went close on all three domestic fronts, but, heartbreakingly, finished the season empty-handed.

Tottenham Hotspur 5 v West Ham United 0

League Cup fifth round replay
Monday 2 February 1987

White Hart Lane
Attendance 41,995

The son of a Spurs double winner tears the hammers apart on his way to a record-breaking goalscoring season

Teams

David Pleat	**Managers**	John Lyall
Ray Clemence	1	Phil Parkes
Danny Thomas	2	Billy Bonds
Mitchell Thomas	3	George Parris
		(Sub. Paul Hilton)
Richard Gough	4	Tony Gale
Gary Mabbutt	5	Alvin Martin
Ossie Ardiles	6	Neil Orr
Glenn Hoddle	7	Mark Robson
Paul Allen	8	Alan Devonshire
Nico Claesen	9	Mark Ward
Clive Allen	10	Frank McAvennie
Chris Waddle	11	Tony Cottee
Claesen 6, Hoddle 71 Clive Allen 80, pen 86, 89	**Scorers**	

Referee: V Callow

FORTY-NINE GOALS in one season. When your playing career is over, nearly every player has one memory that sticks in the mind, in some cases it's a particular game or a magical moment, but I'm delighted to say mine is a whole season!

Nearly everybody I know remembers me for scoring 49 goals in the 1986/87 season and people still ask me about it a lot today; particularly Tottenham fans, but also fans who don't support Spurs, which is always quite flattering.

What made the achievement so special was the fact that it was so rare for a striker to score 40 goals in one season in the top division – even in those days. I think Ian Rush reached the 40-mark one season and Andy Cole managed it in the early-90s for Newcastle, but to get nearly 50 is unthinkable these days and something I will certainly never forget.

Because I scored so many goals that season it's very difficult for me to pick out a single game. I scored twice in nine separate games and got three hat-tricks, so on a personal level, many of those games were special. As a team, we were also very successful, reaching the League Cup semi-final, the FA Cup final and finishing third in the league, so you could take your pick from any number of big games from among the 57 we played that season. Imagine if we'd been playing in Europe as well!

If I have to pick one, though, the game that springs to mind is the League Cup quarter-final replay against West Ham at White Hart Lane, when I scored a nine-minute, second-half hat-trick.

Although for most people, the most memorable game from that season was the classic FA Cup final, which we lost 3-2 to Coventry, the memories from that match aren't particularly happy ones for me. And even though the League Cup also ended in disappointment after three dramatic games against Arsenal in the semi-final, it was the competition in which I was most prolific. I still hold the record for the number of League Cup goals in one season, and this at a time when every club took it as seriously as every other competition and always played their strongest side. I scored 12 in nine games in the Littlewoods Cup – as it was then called – breaking the previous record held jointly by Geoff Hurst and Rodney Marsh, who scored his 11 goals in 1967 when he played alongside my father, Les Allen, in Queen's Park Rangers's League Cup-winning side.

As many Spurs fans will know, my father was the inside-left when Bill Nicholson's great side won the double in 1960/61 and dad always hoped I would follow in his footsteps and play for the club.

I joined Spurs as a schoolboy, but I decided to start my professional career at Queen's Park Rangers, where my dad had been manager from 1968 to 1971. It was a decision we made together, based on the fact that I would get my first-team opportunity young – at just 18 – whereas that probably wouldn't have happened at Spurs, who were a much bigger club, full of established internationals. I was the young kid in an ageing QPR side and the experience did me the world of good. Spurs would track me for a number of years before I finally re-signed for them and it was quite a journey back to White Hart Lane.

I scored over 30 goals at Loftus Road in just one season in the first team before I joined Arsenal in the summer of 1980 for £1,250,000 – which was a pretty big deal at the time. I think my dad was quite disappointed that Spurs didn't come in for me at this point – and that I joined Arsenal of all teams! But I actually ended up playing just three pre-season games for Arsenal; the first against Rangers at home, the others against Red Star Belgrade and Vasco da Gama on a mini pre-season tour. On returning from that trip I was immediately shipped out to Crystal Palace in a swap deal that saw left-back Kenny Sansom go the other way.

People couldn't understand what had gone on. I was at Highbury for just 63 days! There was lots of speculation and several different theories were put forward. One was that Crystal Palace wanted to buy me, but didn't have the cash to pay QPR directly, whereas Arsenal did, and they really wanted Kenny, so came to an arrangement. If so, why didn't they just buy him straight from Palace?! There was no foundation to any of these rumours, but it was quite an experience to be involved in!

The one thing I said at the time was that I didn't want it to affect the most important thing to me: playing football. I'd just turned 19 and my short few weeks at Highbury was a great experience. I was surprised, yes, but disappointed, no. I could understand Terry Neill's thinking. If Arsenal's priority was to bring Kenny in, and the only way they could do the deal was by sending me to Palace, what can you do?

Anyway, Terry Venables, who I really enjoyed working with, left Selhurst Park shortly after I joined and I had a difficult time under the new manager – a guy called Ernie Walley! After just one season I ended up back at QPR, where I was much happier.

I continued to score goals for Rangers and, in June 1984, Spurs finally came in for me. It was one of the only times I saw my father quite emotional.

Spurs were always very close to his heart and he used to take me to games in the early '70s, when the Glory Glory Boys were challenging for honours, particularly in Europe, so I grew up supporting them.

When I returned, they'd just won the UEFA Cup for a second time, which was a magnificent achievement, so I was joining a very good side. I was 24, knew a lot of the players from representing England at various levels and I just felt it was my destiny to join Spurs – it was what I really wanted. I'd always felt very comfortable and very at home there, so much so that when I signed, I remember Peter Shreeves, the manager at the time, saying to me, "I'm sure you know where the ground is Clive, I'll see you in the morning."

People point to the fact that I only had one good season at Spurs – and I must admit, to score that many goals was a complete one-off – but I didn't have a bad record in my other three seasons at White Hart Lane, especially if you consider the circumstances...

I got off to the best possible start, scoring twice on the opening day of the 1984/85 season in a 4-1 win at eventual champions Everton. I also scored twice against my old club QPR in September and twice more against Stoke in October. In fact, up to that point, I'd got all my Spurs goals in twos! Other high points that season included winning goals against Liverpool in both the League Cup and the FA Cup and a goal in each leg of the UEFA Cup third-round clash with Bruges. In all, I scored 10 goals in 20 games during my first season, a pretty good return if you consider that I never really had an extended run in the team.

Steve Archibald and Alan Brazil had departed for pastures new during the summer I joined the club, which left Garth Crooks and Mark Falco as the first-choice strike partnership and to be fair they scored 47 goals between them that season, so I couldn't really complain about being on the bench.

As for the team itself, many people believe we should have won the title that season, and they're probably right. After an up and down start (seven wins, five losses and just one draw from the opening 13 games), we lost just once in 17 league games. But then we lost four of the next six matches, including a match we should have won comfortably at home to eventual champions Everton, and our title challenge faded.

The next season, 1985/86, was a frustrating one for me. Again, my goalscoring record wasn't too bad – 13 in 30 – but I'd been plagued by a series of groin injuries throughout those first two seasons. I had a few operations and finally got it sorted by spring 1986, when I finished the season with six goals in the last six games. It was the first time I'd been completely injury-free since I'd joined Spurs and, having missed so much of the season, I decided to train all the way through the summer, so that by the time the start of the 1986/87 season came around I was in the best shape of my life.

After finishing a disappointing tenth that season, Peter Shreeves was sacked as manager and replaced by David Pleat, who had worked wonders with Luton Town on limited resources. I had known Peter since I had trained with Spurs as a schoolboy. He was a very good coach and I always enjoyed playing for him, but the board felt a more attacking approach was needed, which as a striker is something you always welcome. David Pleat's reputation as an all-out attacking manager stemmed from Luton's free-scoring early '80s side including the likes of Brian Stein, Paul Walsh and David Moss. His catchphrase was "attack and be damned"!

The first thing David did was freshen up Spurs' squad a bit. Graham Roberts, Paul Miller and Mark Falco soon left, with Richard Gough, Mitchell Thomas, Steve Hodge and the Belgian striker Nico Claesen brought in.

We began the season playing 4-4-2 with myself and Nico forming a new striker partnership and from a personal point of view the season couldn't have started better. I scored a hat-trick in our 3-0 opening day win at Villa Park, one more in a draw at home to Newcastle two days later, and from there I never looked back. By November I was averaging a goal a game, but the problem was, nobody else was finding the net. In fact, by November only one other player – Graham Roberts – had scored for us in the league. When I went three games without scoring – and we lost all three – David decided it was time for a change. He stuck with the usual 4-4-2 for the home win against Coventry – I scored the only goal – while we worked on a new formation in training.

I remember after about ten games Ian St John and Jimmy Greaves having a bit of banter on their influential *Saint & Greavsie* show [ITV's Saturday lunchtime rival to the BBC's *Football Focus*], with Ian suggesting that I was going to break Jimmy's Spurs record of 46 goals in one season. I remember being interviewed about this and saying that I would love to break it, but that, even though I'd got off to a flyer, I didn't think it would be possible, because I would have to continue going at a goal a game throughout the season and hope that we would have a good run in at least one of the cups and remain injury free. It was a lot to ask.

Now, it's rare that a striker will welcome being played up front on his own – ask most strikers and they'll tell you they would much rather play with a partner – and you would perhaps expect to get fewer chances (making Greavsie's record even more difficult to beat), but in my case it actually upped my goal rate.

With Glenn Hoddle given a free role in a new-look five-man midfield, and Chris Waddle, my cousin Paul Allen, Ossie Ardiles, Steve Hodge and Tony Galvin also providing plenty of creativity, suddenly we were full of goals. After scoring twice in a 4-2 win at Oxford on the new formation's first outing, I just couldn't stop scoring. I scored 12 goals in eight games during that period, the final brace coming in a 4-3 defeat to Coventry, funnily enough. Of course, that wouldn't prove to be the thriller against Coventry that everybody remembers from that season.

It was a brave decision of David's to go with five in midfield as it was a completely new innovation in English football, but the season just took off for us after that. We were playing with such free spirit, such fluidity, that, even though we were conceding goals as well, particularly away from home, we were always confident we could score more goals than the other team. The approach suited the personnel we had, so David didn't see any reason to change it.

With Nico Claesen injured, we had no other recognised strikers, so David analysed the players he had and devised a system that worked. That was one of his great strengths and it certainly got the best out of me. I don't know why it suited me so well. Perhaps it meant that I could play on the shoulder of the last defender and make the runs I wanted to make knowing that nobody else would be doing the same and crowding my space. The midfield players scored the majority of their goals by running from deep and arriving late in the box.

I also had great service, of course. Glenn was given a free role with very little defensive responsibility and he was absolutely fantastic. That role suited him perfectly and, with his sublime passing, he must have provided me with about 80 percent of my chances that season. We really played to each other's individual strengths.

We were in the middle of a tremendous run of eight wins in nine games when we faced West Ham in the fifth round of the League Cup in late January.

We'd thumped them 4-0 in the league at White Hart Lane on Boxing Day, when I got another brace, but they were always going be a different proposition at Upton Park and they would be out for revenge. Spurs versus West Ham always had a bit of spice and the fact that cousin Paul used to play for them gave it that extra bit of needle. With the game postponed because of a frozen pitch six days earlier, there was even more anticipation when we finally did lock horns on a Tuesday night in East London and, as expected, it was a lot closer than our previous encounter.

Glenn and I both had early efforts cleared off the line and we finally got the goal we deserved when Paul slipped me through and I fired past Phil Parkes. West Ham came out firing in the second half and I remember Richard Gough made a tremendous goal-line clearance from Scottish striker Frank McAvennie. But a few minutes later his partner in crime Tony Cottee pounced after Alan Dickens's shot was blocked. It was end to end after that, but a draw was probably a fair result, although we weren't too disappointed as we now had the chance to take them back to the Lane, where we'd won five on the bounce and were confident of finishing the job.

As was often the case in those days, the replay was the very next week, six days later, in fact, on a Monday night, straight after our 4-0 fourth round FA Cup victory over Second Division Crystal Palace. It was always a big game against West Ham, especially under lights. Don't ask me why, but the atmosphere was always that extra bit special for night games at White Hart Lane, and we expected another open, but fiercely-fought, derby.

Despite the success we'd had playing a fluid 4-5-1, the manager actually reverted back to 4-4-2 for the replay, with the fit again Nico Claesen returning alongside me up front. Tony Galvin dropped to the bench with Chris Waddle moving across to the left wing; it was a very attack-minded formation.

For West Ham, their goalscorer from the first leg, midfielder Alan Dickens, was injured, while Tony Gale returned alongside Alvin Martin at the centre of their defence and veteran Billy Bonds made his first start for nearly two years in place of the injured Ray Stewart.

A 5-0 win suggests the game was very one-sided and in the end we did play really well and deserved to win emphatically, but the scoreline doesn't tell the whole story. In fact, it was West Ham who made the early running and Billy Bonds of all people, playing at right-back, had their two best chances. I distinctly remember the second one, which he somehow managed to head over from about two yards out.

Had they been in front, West Ham could easily have sat back and made life very difficult for us, but we survived and, after those early scares, we managed to get an early goal of our own. Ossie Ardiles – who, can you believe, was supposed to be our most defensive midfielder that night?! – strode forward and slid the ball through to Nico Claesen, who swept it past Phil Parkes into the corner. It was a clinical finish and you could say David's decision to change things was immediately vindicated.

With a goal lead and the crowd behind us, we felt confident of going on to win the game, but despite enjoying the majority of possession and creating several chances, we knew better than to think West Ham would just lie down. We just couldn't get that second goal and with such a slender lead, you do wonder whether it's going to be one of those nights. And, of course, there is always the danger you will get hit by the sucker punch.

Thankfully, West Ham rarely threatened, we kept plugging away, and with 20 minutes left, we finally made another breakthrough. Glenn Hoddle, so often the provider, got on the scoresheet himself, It effectively put the game beyond West Ham and we could now afford to turn on the style. Of course, I didn't expect the game to unfold as spectacularly for me as it did...

Although I took the plaudits for my quickfire hat-trick, the real Man of the Match that night was my cousin Paul, who was playing on our right wing. As I mentioned earlier, he made his name with West Ham, becoming the youngest player to appear in an FA Cup final as a 17 year-old in 1980, before joining Spurs in 1985, a year later than me.

Despite his success at Upton Park, he was given a bit of stick whenever he returned and the first game of this tie had been no different. He was obviously pumped up playing against his old club and he had one of his best games for Spurs in the replay. In the second half in particular he was unbelievable and the way my hat-trick came about made it in an extra special night: he created all three.

The first came ten minutes from time. Paul beat his full-back, George Parris, and I managed to get in front of my marker and turn the ball in. The second, in the 86th minute, was a penalty, which Paul won, again after outwitting the West Ham defence. For the third, he cut in from the right at pace, slid the ball through perfectly for me and all I had to do was apply the finishing touch.

As I celebrated my hat-trick, I will always remember running over to him and lifting his arms up in the air as if to say, "that's your goal – and your night – as much as mine." I was delighted for myself, delighted for him and obviously delighted for the team that we were through to the semi-finals. Little did we know, it would be the high point of our season.

To the neutral observer it was our three games in the semi-final – two legs and a replay – that were most memorable from that League Cup run. They were classic North London derbies, all played under lights, all very fiercely contested. And on a personal level they were all memorable for me too, as I opened the scoring in each game, the second leg being the game in which I broke the League Cup goalscoring record. When I reflect back on that semi-final I still can't believe that we lost...

I scored the only goal of the game at Highbury in the first leg and then gave us the lead at White Hart Lane, which put us firmly in the driving seat. It emerged later that at half-time the Spurs stadium announcer told fans over the tannoy how they could buy tickets for the final! I don't know whether that fired Arsenal up or not, but we certainly never thought the job was done. They eventually got the equaliser, then scored a dramatic winner on the night in the last minute of normal time. Neither side could find a decisive goal in extra-time and, after winning a toss of the coin, David Pleat unsurprisingly decided to play the replay at home, where we were particularly strong.

Again I scored early and again we held on for most of the game until Arsenal equalised – this time in strange circumstances. We were six minutes from Wembley – and the closer you get the more you think about it – when Charlie Nicholas, Arsenal's main goal threat, turned his ankle and had to go off. That meant left-winger Ian Allison came on and he only went and scored with his first touch.

Then in the last minute, a through-ball took a wicked deflection off Danny Thomas's heel straight into the path of midfielder David Rocastle, who ran on to score the winner. It was the only time Arsenal had been ahead in the tie and we were left wondering what might have been. Like I said, I don't know how we lost.

Three days later, in a league game against Queen's Park Rangers at the Lane, Danny's career was ended by injury after a tackle by Gavin Maguire, while Charlie Nicholas returned from his injury for the League Cup final against Liverpool and scored both Arsenal's goals in a 2-1 win in the game which ended Ian Rush's incredible record of Liverpool never having lost a match in which he had scored. It just shows you what a bizarre and cruel game football can be sometimes.

By the time we'd gone out of the League Cup, we were also in the quarter-finals of the FA Cup, a competition in which I wasn't as prolific. As long as the team were winning, though, I didn't mind, and two great goals from Chris and Glenn at Plough Lane put us into the semis at the expense of Wimbledon. A week later we beat Liverpool 1-0 at home. They were still fighting with us for second place in the league, with Everton now way out in front. In fact, a slip-up against Luton aside, our form was very good going into the semi-final where we destroyed a decent Watford side 4-1 at Villa Park. Paul and I both got on the scoresheet and I remember him turning to me at half-time and saying, "I can't believe this, the semi-final of the FA Cup and we're 3-0 up!" I just looked at him and said: "We've not won it yet." But we were soon 4-0 ahead and, although another member of the Allen family – my cousin Malcolm – pulled one back, we were on our way to Wembley.

My previous experiences with Spurs and FA Cup finals had been bad ones. I was in the QPR side when we played Keith Burkinshaw's team in the 1982 Final but, as Graham Roberts alluded to in his chapter, I had to limp off early in the first game and wasn't fit enough to return for the replay, which we lost to a Glenn Hoddle penalty. That was another prolific season for me and I'd like to think I could have made a difference in that final.

Fast forward five years and everybody was convinced we would beat Coventry. They were a decent side, and the league games had finished with both home sides winning by a single goal margin, but we'd beaten similar standard opposition in Wimbledon and Watford on the way to the final and after challenging Liverpool and Everton in the league and going so close in the League Cup we just felt it was going to be our year. Beause Spurs won the Cup in '61, '62 and '67 some people also thought we were destined to repeat the trick in the '80s. But later, when you sat down and analysed our 3-2 defeat, it almost feels like it was Coventry who were destined to win it.

Don't get me wrong, it was one of the most disappointing experiences of my career – if not the most disappointing experience – especially after I'd given us the dream start, heading in Chris Waddle's cross in the second minute, but it just wasn't to be. We did everything we could to win that game, and played some brilliant football on the day as we had throughout the campaign, but that's the magic of the competition. If you're destined to win it, you will. Twice Coventry pegged us back and for them to win it with that bizarre own goal from Mabbsy... well, there's nothing you can do about that.

Some people have suggested we lacked a bit of grit, something that has been levelled against Tottenham teams since the '60s really, and because the club has a tradition of playing with style, I suppose digging in wasn't our forté. But we certainly had characters in our team; it was more a case of not quite being able to close games out. Only Glenn, Clem and Ossie really had that experience of winning things.

On a personal level, the 1986/87 season was the best of my career, almost the perfect season. As recognition of my goalscoring exploits, I was named Footballer of the Year by the Football Writers and Player of the Year by the PFA, both huge individual honours and something I'm extremely proud of. But would I trade in those awards and 10 goals for a trophy? Yes. Absolutely. To be perfectly honest, I would probably have traded in 20 of those goals for a major trophy as I never won one during my career. To miss out completely after going close on three fronts was heartbreaking and our style of football alone almost merited a trophy. You could say the season was like a perfect move that just lacked a finish – something I'd managed to apply with great regularity throughout the season.

You might say we were victims of our own success. We played 57 games and in those days you didn't have huge squads; I played in 52 of those games and some of lads even more. But because the games come thick and fast you never really think about it at the time. By the turn of the year we were literally rolling from game to game, with very little training in between. In fact, because of our success in cup compettiions, our run in to the end of the league season and build up to the FA Cup final saw us play 13 games in 42 days – that's every four days over a sustained period! But there was a real momentum, something that only really stopped at the final hurdle, so I wouldn't blame tiredness.

On top of those 52 games I was also recalled to the England squad by Bobby Robson that season. In February, I sat on the bench in Madrid as Gary Lineker scored all four goals in a 4-2 friendly win against Spain. It was during that game that I realised he would always be first choice, no matter how well I was playing at Spurs and how many goals I was scoring, and his international record speaks for itself. Saying that, at the end of April 1987 I actually partnered Gary in the European Championship qualifier in Turkey in place of the injured Peter Beardsley. I scored in that game, but the goal was ruled out because Gary was in an offside position. I'll always hold that against him! Ha, ha!! Funnily enough, it was Gary who would ultimately replace me at Spurs a year after I'd left.

It was to be a disappointing final season for me at Tottenham. I genuinely believe that, had that group of players from the 1986/87 season stayed together under David Pleat, we had a very good chance of going one better the following season and winning something. But Glenn Hoddle left for Monaco – and with him went the source of the majority of my goals – and centre-half Richard Gough joined Rangers just weeks into the new season. We still started well enough, losing just one of our first eight games with me among the goals again, but our form had already begun to suffer when a series of allegations by *The Sun* over his private life forced David to resign in October.

My old Palace boss Terry Venables took over and, although he would eventually win the FA Cup with Spurs in 1991, he struggled with results at first as he set about building a new team. An injury-plagued campaign for Chris Waddle, who was now our most creative player in Glenn's absence, certainly didn't help my own form. I managed 13 goals in 34 games – by no means a drought, but I obviously wasn't as prolific as I would have liked. I was out of contract at the end of the season and joined Bordeaux for £1,000,000. It was good money for Spurs and a new challenge for me.

It would be 16 years before I rejoined Spurs – as part of the backroom staff – where I'm now the development coach. Even the young lads at Spurs, some of who weren't even born, know about that season and the fact that I scored 49 goals, which is nice. I suppose in a way it helps you to earn their respect, because they know you've been there and done it and know how they are feeling. I would never suggest to the strikers amongst them that they should be scoring that many goals in a season, because I know how hard scoring goals is, but it's nice to be able to pass on my experiences. It's certainly a season I'll never forget.

GARY MABBUTT
DEFENDER 1982–1998

BORN 23 August 1961, Bristol
SIGNED 11 August 1982 from Bristol Rovers; £105,000
SPURS CAREER 626 games, 37 goals
HONOURS UEFA Cup Winner 1984, FA Cup winner 1991, FA Cup runner-up 1987, Charity Shield winner 1991
LEFT Retired 31 May 1998

You'd be hard pushed to find a more consummate professional and football diplomat than Spurs centre-half, Gary Mabbutt. Signed from Bristol Rovers in 1982, the ascendant England U21 player made his debut against Liverpool in the 1982 Charity Shield and gathered credit with each passing performance. He later became team captain and earned 16 full international caps. More impressively, he was awarded an MBE in 1994. His work as a diabetic operating in top level sport was an inspiration to many other sufferers, though he was a pretty nifty footballer too, securing the Spurs back line, most notably amidst manager David Pleat's attacking frenzy in 1987. He also picked up a number of honours with the team, including a UEFA Cup winner's medal in 1984.

Tottenham Hotspur 2 v Nottingham Forest 1 (after extra time)

FA Cup Final
Saturday 18 May 1991

Wembley Stadium
Attendance 80,000

'Gazzamania' takes on a new meaning at Wembley as Spurs see off Nottingham Forest

Teams

Terry Venables	**Managers**	Brian Clough
Erik Thorsvedt	1	Mark Crossley
Justin Edinburgh	2	Gary Charles
Pat van den Hauwe	3	Stuart Pearce
Steve Sedgley	4	Des Walker
David Howells	5	Steve Chettle
Gary Mabbutt	6	Roy Keane
Paul Stewart	7	Gary Crosby
Paul Gascoigne (Sub. Nayim)	8	Garry Parker
Vinny Samways (Sub. Paul Walsh)	9	Nigel Clough
Gary Lineker	10	Lee Glover (Sub. Brian Laws)
Paul Allen	11	Ian Woan (Sub. Steve Hodge)
Stewart 55, Walker (og) 94	**Scorers**	Pearce 16

Referee: R Milford

I WOULD SAY THAT it was a funny time for Spurs in 1991, because leading up to the FA Cup final that year we were probably on the financial pages as much as we'd been on the back pages. There were a lot of things happening with the club off the pitch, and a lot of financial troubles were being thrown into the mixer [take-over bids were the order of the day at White Hart Lane with Alan Sugar later taking over Tottenham Hotspur PLC in a joint venture with Terry Venables, though the club was £20 million in debt].

People always talk about the money troubles and the financial problems at the club at that time. Fans always ask whether that affected us, but the truth is, it didn't. The playing side of the club completely disassociated itself from the financial problems of Tottenham Hotspur.

In fact, I think our success in the FA Cup that year came as a reaction to what was going on elsewhere. All the negative things that were being written about the club could be forgotten and the players and fans could concentrate on the cup run. It worked too: the football side moved along without too much interference and the FA Cup run acted as the perfect distraction. As players, we could see what was going on off the pitch, but we had other things to focus on.

It was business as usual as far as we were concerned. I'm not really sure whether (manager) Terry Venables kept us informed on the situation as it went along or not, but it certainly didn't seem to have any effect on the side. If anything it had a positive effect. All this stuff was going on but we were determined to carry on regardless. We wanted to keep it as business as usual at White Hart Lane.

But even before the final there had been some wonderful games in that FA Cup run. The semi-final against Arsenal on 14 April at Wembley was a memorable match in itself, mainly because it was the first semi-final to be held at the famous old stadium. It still amazes me that, even today, it's the game people talk about. Every single Spurs supporter will talk more fondly of the semi-final victory than the FA Cup final itself! For them, beating Arsenal is always a highlight, especially in the manner that we did, but for the players it's completely different. For us, beating Arsenal in the semi-final was really just a means to an end: we had to win to get to the FA Cup final. If we'd gone on and lost in the final, the win against Arsenal would have meant nothing to us. As it was, Arsenal were going for the double that season, they were in form, miles ahead in the league, and they were clear favourites that day because we hadn't been enjoying a very good run of form up until that game.

And yet, on the day, we put in a magnificent performance. Especially Paul Gascoigne who scored with a wonderful 30 yard free-kick past David Seaman. That goal set the tempo, but that was another story in itself and getting through that game gave the whole club a huge lift.

Then, of course, came the final against Nottingham Forest. Now, it was my second Cup final and the first one in 1987 had been tinged with sadness, not only because we'd lost 3-2 to Coventry City, but because I'd scored an own goal in the process that ultimately decided the game. I did actually score a goal at the right end in that game, but nobody seems to remember that.

That was probably the lowest point in my career, but, tongue in cheek, it's made me an absolute legend in the Midlands. There's even a Coventry fanzine named after me – it's called GMK, or *Gary Mabbutt's Knee*. I think I've got free food and drink for life in the Midlands because of that.

I remember that game so clearly, though. From the playing point of view we were clear favourites to win beforehand. The club had never been beaten in an FA Cup final in it's history. If we'd have played anything like our capabilities we would have won against Coventry, but, as it was, we lost Spurs' first FA Cup final ever.

Having said that, it was more frustrating because it was my first FA Cup final and to lose it the way we did was a huge disappointment. It's never nice to score an own goal, least of all in a Cup final, but I always tell myself that it was just one of those things. The own goal was unfortunate and it couldn't have been helped. I put my leg up to block a cross. Ninety-nine times out of 100 it would have gone out for a corner. On this one timely occasion the ball flew across, looped over our keeper, Ray Clemence, and lost us the Cup final. It happens, but it was hugely disappointing.

Things had actually been going quite well that day, too – Clive Allen had put us in the lead early on with one of the many goals he'd scored that season; 49 in total. Then Coventry equalised. I scored at the other end, before Keith Houchen levelled again with a famous diving header. Then, of course, came the own goal, but it was a cracking game for the neutral.

Come the 1991 FA Cup Final I wanted to lay those ghosts to rest. The night before the game we stayed in the Royal Lancaster Hotel overlooking Hyde Park. I was sharing a room with Gary Lineker and it was a very relaxed preparation. We got up earlyish in the morning and me and Gary went for a stroll around Hyde Park, which was nice. We were calm. I wasn't nervous. It appeared that most of the players were quite relaxed, even when we were getting on the coach and going to Wembley.

I remember it seemed like every other car on the road was on its way to Wembley. There were Spurs fans everywhere, tooting their horns, but you get excited rather than fearful at that stage in the day. It was passionate, but there was no Wimbledon-style craziness the night before, or on the day for that matter.

We had a good side going into that Cup final. The season had already been marked as Paul Gascoigne's swansong because he was due to go to Lazio in the summer, but Gary Lineker was in good form that season, as were Paul Stewart, Erik Thorsvedt and Steve Sedgley, as well as Vinny Samways. It was a really good side. But really, Paul Gascoigne was our weapon. It's not possible for one man to get a team to a Cup final on his own, but Gazza very nearly did just that.

He scored against Oxford in the early rounds and against Portsmouth... all the way through that cup run, Paul was on the top of his game in every single match that he played. He really was magnificent in the cup build up. After his amazing goal at Wembley and we'd beaten Arsenal in the semi, Paul really made us favourites to win the trophy. It was as if our name was on the cup.

The opposition that day were tough, though. Brian Clough's teams always were. Cloughie had never won an FA Cup and a lot of hype was flying around that maybe it was his turn to win it with Nottingham Forest, but Terry Venables hadn't won a domestic trophy of any kind up until that stage, so the build up between the two managers was incredible. But as they both walked out on to the pitch, they did so hand in hand. It was an amazing moment.

We walked out onto the pitch and they were just in front of me. But the thing that hit me at that moment wasn't the pair of them holding hands, it was the atmosphere. As captain, you're the first person that the fans see and the roar that hits you at Wembley with a full house on Cup final day is amazing. It was a special moment that I'll remember for the rest of my life.

Of course, once you're on the pitch you've got all the dignitaries to get through and that takes about 15 minutes. All the players want to get on with the game and get down to business – you just can't wait for the game to begin. But in the first half of that match everything that possibly could have gone wrong for us, did. It was a disaster. Everything we tried, didn't seem to work and everything Forest did, seemed to fall their way. Disaster number one – the most famous – was the terrible situation with Paul Gascoigne, where he committed two really bad fouls and injured himself in the process. This led him to being stretchered off and missing out on pretty much the whole game.

I remember the first tackle simply because I didn't see it. Gazza cleared the ball in front of me and, as he did so, carried on with his boot and caught Forest's Garry Parker just below the chest. But as he kicked the ball, I became distracted. I followed the flight of his clearance and didn't even see Paul's follow through. This is a natural reaction as a defender. Your first instinct is to see whether the ball has been cleared away to safety. I didn't see that Paul had continued his challenge and left his foot up, hurting Parker in the process.

When the referee blew up for a free-kick, I was totally confused. What normally happens when somebody clears the ball is that the player coming into the challenge can leave his foot there and foul the clearing player. That's what I thought had happened: as Gazza cleared the ball, I thought Garry Parker must have caught Paul in his follow through, not the other way round. I thought it was a free-kick to us. In reality it was for Forest.

I then had to get back into position to organise the free-kick and sort the defence out. But had I actually witnessed what had happened I would made a point of having had a word with Paul. It would have been my job to calm him down because it was such a bad challenge. But I didn't see it. I didn't know what he'd done. And I didn't actually see it until I saw the replay on the telly much later. That could have changed things.

I got back into the wall. Everything was organised, everyone was marking their man. And we cleared the free-kick. Then, five minutes later, exactly the same thing happened. Gary Charles came running across me and Paul went in for a challenge. It really was an atrocious tackle. He caught him so badly. But the sad fact was that it ended Paul's FA Cup final – he'd damaged his ligaments in making the tackle – and he was soon stretchered off. Fortunately, Gary Charles wasn't too badly injured, but he was lucky though, because it was such a bad challenge.

A lot of fury followed that tackle. Paul managed to get back up on his feet for the ensuing free-kick and placed himself in the wall. The ball was about twenty yards outside the box. I was on the end of the wall to try to provide a block on the shot when the free-kick came in. I remember Stuart Pearce stepped up to take it and if you watch the video now you'll see that as he makes his run up towards the ball, the Forest central defender puts both hands on my shoulders and pulls me to the floor. As I'm going down I can remember seeing the ball passing me. I'm on the ground as the ball hits the back of our net.

I remember looking up at the referee, Roger Milford, in the hope that he had seen the foul, but I knew as soon as I saw him running back to the centre circle that he'd given a goal. So we were one-nil down and from the kick-off, Paul collapsed in a heap. There was absolutely no way he was fit to continue, but we didn't panic as he was stretchered off and replaced with Nayim. Players are quite stoical really. When things like that happen we just get on with it and deal with the problem. There's no time to think, "Paul's gone off, we've blown it." You just move on. But saying that, it was a huge blow because Paul had been so influential throughout the whole FA Cup competition.

With Gazza off and a goal conceded, it got worse: we had a perfectly good goal disallowed. Gary Lineker put the ball away, but the offside flag went up, even though there was no way he was offside.

Later he went round the goalkeeper, Mark Crossley, ready to put the ball in the back of the net, when the keeper brought him down. The ref awarded a penalty, but rather than scoring and levelling the game, Gary missed the ensuing spot-kick as the keeper saved. So literally, everything went wrong.

That incident was hugely controversial. Today, a lot of people say to me that Paul Gascoigne should have been sent off for his two tackles. If that was the case we would have been down to ten men for much of the game and might not have won the FA Cup. But I always say that the Forest keeper should have also gone off when he pulled down Gary. He'd gone round him and was about to put the ball away when Crossley brought him down, which was a sending off offence – or at least it is today. All things considered, I'd rather have an outfield player sent off than a goalkeeper. I think maybe the referee was right not to send anyone off in that game, though.

At half-time, with all those factors running against us it looked pretty bad, especially with Gascoigne – our talisman – stretchered off. In the dressing room, Terry Venables gave his best team talk ever. He hardly said a word.

He basically told us to forget the first half and to keep playing the way we were. It was so simple, but it was right. We hadn't played badly, things just hadn't gone our way. He reiterated that we were playing well and that we'd been unlucky. He didn't want the bad luck to affect our play. He wanted us to perform exactly the same way in the second half. He knew if we played like that again, we could turn the game around.

Terry was a brilliant coach. He was great with the players. His coaching is his main attribute and that year he was totally focused on coaching the team, building the squad and getting our play right on the field. It showed in our performances that year. That season, he got us working so well.

So the game plan was, "Don't change anything." And that's exactly what we did – we carried on regardless.

In the second half, Paul Stewart equalised for us with a great shot after being played in on the right-hand side of the box – I'll always remember his celebration. He ran past the goal, jumped over a hoarding and ran towards the fans. But the hard work wasn't over because that goal only got us into extra-time, but we were on the up.

We came good too, winning it after the extra half an hour. I'll always remember our winning goal. We had a corner on the right hand side and with Terry we always worked on different moves in training from set pieces. It was something he was very good at. Basically, from a corner we would try to create space in the box for our players to exploit.

I ran in front of Gary Lineker and then ran back past him. I was being marked by Des Walker and as I ran back past Gary, he blocked him off. So I managed to get a yard on Des just as the ball was being knocked into the box. I ran round to the far post and as the ball came across I realised it was heading straight for me. I must have been six yards out and I was just about to head the ball into the net when, at the last second, Des flung himself at it in a last ditch attempt to stop me from scoring. The ball rocketed off his head into the top corner.

It was so ironic given what had happened to me in 1987. The fact that it was me standing there, waiting for an opportunity to score the winning goal before Des came in and scored an own goal into the very same net that decided the match... well, it was a weird coincidence.

We played out the game quite well. We were in control, we knew they were going to throw everything at us and it would be tough. Forest had a good side – Steve Hodge, Nigel Clough, Stuart Pearce and a young Roy Keane were all playing – they were strong opposition. But I never really felt that we'd lose after getting our noses in front.

When the final whistle went it was such an outpouring of relief. I think I just ran to the rest of the team. I think the first person I got to was Gary Lineker – it was his first FA Cup win too, because he'd been involved in a defeat for Everton against Liverpool a few years previously. We were all celebrating together on the field and I went over to shake hands with all the Forest players and Brian Clough.

I remember I didn't really talk to Des Walker, despite the similarities in our Cup finals. I knew what he was going through, so I made a point of going over to him, but I knew saying something of consolation wouldn't have been enough. It had happened to me – and it's one of those things that happens to defenders every now and then – but there's nothing you can say or do to make someone feel better about themselves. It's not a nice feeling when you know your team have lost because of your own goal. Believe me it's worse when that match is the FA Cup final.

We all congregated at the bottom of the Royal Box. We stood there as a team and I was thinking to myself how for all those years when I was growing up, FA Cup final day was such a big event. I'd sit in front of the TV from ten in the morning watching *It's A Cup Final Knockout* and *FA Cup Final Mastermind*, the road to Wembley, the coach journeys... suddenly I was there living it. It was amazing. I was standing there thinking "I'm now going up those stairs to lift the FA Cup." It was a great moment.

Forest went up first to get their runners-up medals, then it was my turn. I went up and Prince Charles and Lady Diana were waiting there to present the trophy, as were the Duke and Duchess of Kent. You register them, but because I was the first up the stairs I wasn't quite sure of the procedure or the protocol: should I shake hands with all of them first and then lift the cup, or should I go straight to the cup? In the end, I thought I'd wait for some sort of movement from them before making a grab for the silverware. Fortunately the Duchess of Kent moved forward and handed me the trophy.

It's funny, even though you've won the cup, you're still trying to think of the correct behaviour in front of the Royal Family. Before the game it's not even something you want to consider because you don't want to tempt fate, but once I'd got the cup I turned and lifted it towards our supporters and it felt incredible. I've got pictures of that moment, in fact there's one on the cover of this book – I've got the biggest smile on my face. The noise when you lift that trophy... you can feel the goose bumps rising.

It's difficult to explain because people always ask you what it feels like. I guess, as a boy the FA Cup represents the Glory Game day in football, but it's so difficult to describe in words what it really feels like, what's going through your head... the experience. It's such a cliché, but it's one of those things you dream about from five years of age.

For me it was a very special moment. I've played for England at Wembley and I've won the UEFA Cup with Spurs, but being captain that day and walking up the Wembley steps and meeting Prince Charles... that's probably one of the best moments of my career. Of course, the boys were in a celebratory mood, so we went off to meet the fans and show them the cup.

We ran around the pitch as all teams do, but it was still tinged with sadness because Paul Gascoigne was already lying in a hospital bed with his leg in plaster. He'd damaged his knee ligaments. We got down to the pitch to find out how he was from the doctors, but everything had to go on without him. So firstly we had to meet the media and have our pictures taken. Once that had finished, we did a lap of honour. Then we got back to the dressing room and it was time to get the full details of what had happened to Paul and discover the extent of his condition.

We decided as a team that we were going to go straight from Wembley to the hospital to see him. I had Paul's medal and we thought we should take the FA Cup on the coach with us so he could get his hands on it for the first time. We knew he'd appreciate the gesture. It also seemed like the right thing to do.

Once we got down there, I walked off the coach with the cup and Paul's medal. All the cameras were there waiting for us and we went straight up to his room. I knocked on the door and walked in with the trophy. Paul was already lying there, heavily bandaged. When we turned up, he got very emotional. He was a very emotional person anyway, but he said he'd watched the game and saw me picking up the cup on TV from his bed not long after he'd got there. It was a very difficult time for him because it was supposed to be his last game for Tottenham before his move to Lazio, but he'd missed out on winning the Cup final with the rest of us. And it was hard for him and us because he had been such a talisman throughout that competition.

All we had to do next was to calm him down. I remember we virtually had to tie him to the bed because he was determined to come to the victory celebrations that were being laid on for us that night. There was a dinner planned, but unfortunately he was in no position to even move, let alone go to a party. I'm sure they had to sedate him to stop him from turning up!

There are so many Gazza stories I could tell you, though. He was such a wonderful person to have around the club. In fact, there are probably more stories I can't repeat than the ones that I actually can! I remember my first experience of his sense of humour came after our first away game after he'd joined from Newcastle, where he had built his reputation as a bit of a character. I was captain of the club and it was clear to us all that Paul was a special talent, but his reputation did precede him.

Anyway, after matches, the players go to the players lounge, but being a diabetic I would go to the coach. Being a pampered soccer star we had chefs on the bus for our journey home. I always had to have an injection after a game and for away games I always went on the coach to take my jabs and eat.

Anyway, I was on my own on the coach and I had my needle out and my insulin vial ready. As I'm putting the insulin into the syringe I saw Paul getting on the coach. He walked all the way to the back of the bus and I saw him clocking me.

"Mabbsy, what are you doing?" he said.

I explained to him that I was a diabetic, but he still seemed confused.

"What do you mean?"

I said, "Well Paul, I have to have four injections every day."

"What? Every day while you're a footballer?"

"No, I have to have four injections every day for the rest of my life."

He looked at me and said incredulously, "Four injections? Every day, Mabbsy? For the rest of your life? Cool. I bet you can't wait to die, can you?"

I looked at him and I could see that cheesy Paul Gascoigne grin spreading across his face. But he was like that all the time. He was a brilliant person to have around the club. That particular season he was at his best – it was probably the best form of his whole career. He would do things in training or on the pitch that you could not believe – tricks, flashes of skill. He was amazing. After matches he was just as entertaining – he was always doing things that were surprising you, but we shouldn't really go in to those too much!

There was no indication before the Cup final that he was over excited though. Nobody could have predicted what he was going to do. Paul was always very pumped up before games. He's huge on emotions anyway and we thought he was just his normal self. Looking back it was a big game for Spurs, an FA Cup final, Paul's first Cup final, his final game for Spurs, the biggest single game in English football... but we felt that he was in exactly the same mood for the semi-final.

There was a big difference, however. In the semi-final he had scored that brilliant free-kick early on. From that moment, all the energy and emotion came out of him after the ball had flown past David Seaman and into the back of the net. In the FA Cup final he didn't do anything to shake off all that excess energy and excitement. It was still in his system. I think he was so tensed up and the adrenaline was pumping so hard that it just got a hold of him.

Throughout the whole of that year Paul was brilliant, but so was the whole team. I look back on it very fondly, especially lifting the cup at Wembley. There was a lot of controversy off the pitch – the financial troubles, Paul's transfer to Lazio – but in the end, the football showed through.

Terry Venables was delighted, too. It was his first major domestic trophy and he deserved it – he was one of the most respected English coaches at that time. It was also Gary Linker's first and only FA Cup victory. And I got to lift the trophy in front of all those Spurs fans. What a memory! You could say it was a very happy office all round.